The Tongue of the Tiger

Rolf D. Cremer

Mary J. Willes

The Tongue Of The Tiger

OVERCOMING LANGUAGE BARRIERS IN INTERNATIONAL TRADE

World Scientific
Singapore • New Jersey • London • Hong Kong

Published by

World Scientific Publishing Co. Pte. Ltd.

P O Box 128, Farrer Road, Singapore 912805

USA office: Suite 1B, 1060 Main Street, River Edge, NJ 07661

UK office: 57 Shelton Street, Covent Garden, London WC2H 9HE

Library of Congress Cataloging-in-Publication Data
A catalog record for this book is available from the Library of Congress.

British Library Cataloguing-in-Publication Data
A catalogue record for this book is available from the British Library.

TONGUE OF THE TIGER

ISBN 981-02-3004-4

This book is printed on acid-free paper.

Printed in Singapore by Uto-Print

To

Beate and Dieter Cremer

Acknowledgements

It is a pleasure to acknowledge the many debts incurred in the course of the research and writing involved in a book like this.

First, we wish to formally thank the owners, directors, and merchandising personnel of the companies, Hong Kong and Macau which provided, from their records, the data we use. Not only did they allow us access to it, imposing no restrictions on its used, they took time to discuss, explain and comment. We acknowledge too the important role played by Flora Seto, our Research Assistant in 1991, and again in 1993-4.

Several institutions contributed, by funding or other forms of support, to a longer term project than we envisaged at its inception. We are indebted to Ricci Island West Ltd., through its support of the China Economic Research Centre based in the University of Macau, to the London University Institute of Education for providing a Visiting Fellowship in 1992-3 and subsequently assisting, by a small grant, the second series of visits to companies and the collection of our Extended Database, to the Chinese University of Hong Kong, and, especially in the final stages, to Massey University, Palmerston North, New Zealand.

We thank Professor Mark Casson, University of Reading, U.K., for permission to quote material written for limited circulation, Drs. Herbert Pierson and Bjorn Jernudd, members of the Editorial Board of the Journal of Asia Pacific Communication, for permission to use material of our own authorship published in that journal, and Mrs. Sandhya Chatterjee for advice on depositing our data in the New Zealand Social Research Data Archive, based at Massey University, and for making information about it accessible on the Internet at this address: http://www.massey.ac.nz.

R D Cremer and M J Willes

Palmerston North, January 1997

Table of Contents

List of Tables and Figures

The common ground of linguistics and economics is communication.

Coulmas, 1991

We do not know enough ... about how we obtain and organize the information needed to communicate appropriately and build agendas across languages and cultures.

Cicourel, 1988

[The existence of transaction costs] implies that methods of coordination alternative to the market, which are themselves costly and in various ways imperfect, may nonetheless be preferable to relying on the pricing mechanism, the only method of coordination normally analyzed by economists.

Coase, 1991

Introduction

This book is about the communicative systems and practices employed in, and indispensable to, the functioning of international trade business in Asia. These systems and practices have been profoundly changed by the advances of telecommunication technology over the last decade. The wider context and overall intention of the book is the discussion of language, especially English, as a key factor in the exemplary export performance of high-performing Asian economies. On this fact, the study brings to bear a different perspective, a novel approach, and the material of a unique database.

The intended readership of this book includes:

- business managers, traders, and students of economics and management;
- researchers in economics, international business, and linguistics; and
- teachers of English for Business Purposes.

The general contention resulting from an interdisciplinary research project undertaken in 1991–94 is that just as factories "run on talk" (Cope and Solomon, 1993), international trade runs on facsimile messages in English between buyers and suppliers. From the perspective of the identified groups of intended readers, this implies three essential propositions on a practical, research and educational level.

- Successful international trading requires a workforce and an organisation of work capable of dealing with the linguistic demands and related cultural barriers which separate and distinguish different markets.
- Economic research can and must put more emphasis on the study of trade and exchange of information between the parties in the context of the actual trade activities of firms. Linguistics provides the required focus on the study of language in the context of purposeful interaction between individuals.

- The teaching of language must recognise and extend the actual strategic language skills that company personnel exercise.

The initial research agenda was to investigate language problems in communication between Asian manufacturers and overseas buyers, with a view to identify errors and mistakes, which could be corrected through better language teaching. This agenda was in several ways complementary to a larger, international project (Institute of Developing Economies, 1984–1990) on the industrial structure of export-oriented, small and medium scale industries in Asia, specifically in Hong Kong and Macau. It used contacts established in the earlier project in order to focus on the day-to-day operations of small, family-owned businesses engaged in international trading in light industrial products, taking textiles and garments in Hong Kong and Macau and dealing with partners worldwide, as an example. At the early stages, the objectives of the research project were therefore remedial in intention, and restricted to what appeared to be a relatively small, practical problem that could be dealt with in isolation. The probable outcome would be some practical suggestions of improvements, such as changes in the design of official forms, and emphasis on specific linguistic problems in language classes.

It soon became clear that the study of the communicative system of international trade transactions, and the language used, was quite a different matter from that initially envisaged, and that we were looking at the detail of processes of small scale coordination that, in the aggregate, make up processes of market exchange, or as Casson (1995) put it:

> "...a process, in which one small step leads on to another, rather than [as] an activity in which there is a single giant leap to a fully coordinated economy. The sequence of steps is not fully optimised as it is within a formal organization where decision-making has been reduced to routine.(...) The apparently uncoordinated nature of coordination does not therefore mean that coordination defies analysis, but rather the analysis of changes in methods of coordination requires a thorough appreciation of the wide ranging implications of information costs." (Casson, 1995:2)

Initial study of the material opened up a new and different perspective on how international trade works. If language, and the exchange of information which it makes possible, is indispensable to international trade, then academic economists, management researchers and managers must make language and communication, in the particular context where it is used, part of their concern. It is a very common requirement, almost standard, in job advertisements, that applicants have the ability to communicate effectively.

With this shift of stance, three decisions concerning the research and this book emerged. Most empirical studies of international trade depend on data more or less heavily aggregated, for example, data on trade volumes, export values, and company profits. Such data do not permit the examination and partial reconstruction of the lowest level, the micro-fabric of the in-company processes that drive international trade.

The first research decision, therefore, was to identify the *deal*, the particular trade transaction, as the unit of investigation, and to compile a sizable database of trade-related text documents that constitute reliable, valid, and objective observations of actual international trade transactions. There can be no doubt about the significance of having access to such micro-level data. The need for such a collection of data has already been authoritatively identified by Ronald Coase in his Nobel Prize lecture in 1991,

> "I have come to the conclusion that the main obstacle faced by researchers of industrial organisation is the lack of data on *contracts and the activities of firms.*" (Coase, 1992: 719),

as has the localised nature of the processes and the mediating function of those who produce and store documents related to the trade transactions they are involved with:

> "Coordination is not effected by a single economy-wide plan of trade (...) it is a localised process implemented in sequential fashion by intermediators who specialise in collecting information for this purpose. This arrangement is a rational response to the costs of collecting and synthesising information." (Casson, 1995: 38)

The problem is that except in very special circumstances, this localised process, i.e. the trade communication within and between companies, is simply not observable.

The indispensability of faxed communication to the process of trading and the retention of these documents in the company files put us into the position to collect a unique and authentic data-set about individual trade transactions. In contrast to data that have been subjected to processes of abstraction and aggregation (and mostly only contain information about prices and quantities), the data collected for this research project consist of text documents generated in the process of actual trade transactions, not for research purposes, but for reference by the trading company. In short, and we will have much more to say about the nature of the database later in Chapter 3, the data consist of retrieved messages which were actually used to monitor and control, in every detail, international trade transactions. These data are reliable and objective, in the sense that they can be, in principle, observed by others, and because they do not depend in any way on the observer's judgment. While we used data from companies in Hong Kong and Macau, the analysis is unlikely to be specific to these locations: the manufacture of light industrial products for exports, especially textiles and garments, is both characteristic and essential for the economic development of the fast growing economies of East and Southeast Asia.

The second decision was to integrate in the treatment of this topic a macro-level, i.e. economic and social aspects; and micro-level, i.e. the actual behaviour and activities of individuals. The study of language and communication in the context of international trade, and the availability of the skills and competencies related to efficient and effective communication, goes far beyond the individual acquisition of useful skills. The experience of the last half century has shown, that international trade, and the ability of countries to compete with their products successfully on the international markets, has been one of the most important factors for countries in achieving sustained economic growth and prosperity. In order to be able to support the international competitiveness of an open economy, it is essential to understand the micro-foundations on which success on the macro-level can be built. The study of language and communication in the context of international trade, or as the title suggests, the Tongue of the Tiger, belongs to these micro-foundations.

Third, we took advantage of an obvious feature of the enquiry, its interdisciplinary character, that allowed our developed interests in economics and linguistics to converge on the topic of international trade communication. Language, in the form of written communication, between the parties of any given international trade transaction, embodies a mirror image of the transaction itself. The communicative systems, the communication technology, the language used, the messages which are exchanged, cannot be separated from the underlying trade deal. The trade deal would not exist, if it were not created on the communicative level in the form of text as well since, as we have said earlier, trade runs on fax.

The Organisation of the Book

All three decisions, and their interconnectedness, are reflected in the organisation of the book. The principal problem of organising an interdisciplinary book about a practical issue is its scope, which ranges across three disciplines, and from macroeconomic and macro-social development issues to the study of trade practices and detailed text analysis.

We have chosen, as an organizing principle, a progressively narrowing focus. Each of the five main chapters offers a focus narrower than the preceding one.

Chapter 1, *Societies and Livelihoods Built on Trade*, aims at establishing empirically the economic and societal context of the contemporary international economy, within which international trade plays an indispensable, dominant and positive role, for successful economic and social development. The obvious rationale for this chapter is to lay out the eminently practical contribution which international trade can make to the development of a country. This, not only an interest in communication, justifies the attention to the details of trade transaction that follows. International trade, in order to be successful, requires an organisational system, within which people and business organisations can interact, to achieve individual and collective goals.

Chapter 2, *The Industrial Organisation of International Trade*, studies the case of Hong Kong and Macau, the organisational make-up of successful trading economies, on the macroeconomic, industry, and company level, thus describing the institutional structure within which the activities of the people who drive trade transactions unfold.

In Chapter 3, *The Language of International Trade Transactions*, the focus narrows to the description and classification of data relating to particular trade transactions encoded in written English and predominantly in the form of facsimile messages. In this chapter and the next two, we are concerned with the fine detail of trade transactions, with the microfabric of international trade, with the activity and interaction of individuals, and specifically with the continuous communication and coordination between buyer and supplier, by which trade deals are initiated, negotiated, monitored, controlled, and finally, brought to completion. The focus on the individual trade transaction, or trade deal, builds directly on the preceding discussion in Chapter 2, on the industrial organisation of trading economies.

Chapter 4 contains *Five Case Studies*. There are two main reasons for the inclusion of case studies. First, it cannot be assumed that outside the group of those immediately concerned with international trade business as part of their daily work, there is a clear and detailed understanding of the orderly sequence common to trade transactions, or of the complexity and variety of its realisations. The case studies are intended to fill this gap, by providing a narrative account of actual trade deals, based on the available data. We hope to illustrate through the case studies what actually must be done by people on the lowest level for international trade to function, given a set of conducive trade policies, favourable market conditions and adequate price signals. Second, the case studies corroborate our claim about the significance of text as the basis for studying international trade transactions. We demonstrate that case studies can be reconstructed entirely from text data, something that would, of course, be impossible to do on the basis of conventional business or trade statistics. The case studies, therefore, demonstrate the particular quality of our database. Text, in particular text encoded in English on facsimile messages, makes it possible for researchers to study any aspect of international trade deals. Of course, the companies have been disguised, because the data on matters like prices, quantities, and business partners are commercially sensitive.

Chapter 5, *Towards a Description of Trade English*, progressively narrows the focus. A selection of text from the database is scrutinised in enough detail to illustrate differences among them and to examine evidence for the view that, from the circumstances of international trade, a new variety of English is emerging. It is not identical to the English taught and learnt in schools throughout Asia, nor with a language imperfectly learnt. It has considerable flexibility in use; it serves the purposes of its users reasonably well, and users have strategies in place for recognising difficulties and resolving them. It is amenable to some preliminary description. Compared with developed varieties of English in use for Air Traffic Control and Ship-to-Shore communication, it is still unsettled and unstable. It is nonetheless recognisable as an operational sub-language for which, on the analogy of SeaSpeak, the English of ship-to-shore communication, (Glover *et al.*,1987) and PoliceSpeak, the language of traffic control in the Channel Tunnel), we use the term *TradeSpeak*.

Finally, the *Conclusion* returns to the broader topics of this *Introduction*. The research is concerned with the texture and the meaning of actual activities, the fabric of lives and livelihoods and the ways in which these can be conceptualised and understood. Such studies do not fit comfortably within the established academic disciplines, yet are indispensable to them. It is quite unsatisfactory simply to say that they are interdisciplinary in their nature. The question of where this study should be located in relation to other fields of study has to be addressed, as have two others, one relating to theoretical implications and practical applications, and the other to further developments.

Chapter 1

Societies and Livelihoods Built on Trade

Whether or not trade is the

> "consequence of a certain propensity [in human nature] to truck, barter, and exchange one thing for another (...) of which no further account can be given",

as Adam Smith (1776: 16) wondered in *The Wealth of Nations*, trade is certainly not an end in itself. The interest in economic exchange in general, and specifically in international trade, derives its justification from the eminently practical contributions it makes to the development of the economy, and therefore, to a people's societal and individual welfare.

Chapter 1 aims at establishing empirically the economic and societal context of the contemporary international economy, within which international trade plays an indispensable, dominant, and positive role for successful economic and social development. It is in this context that we then wish to study the crucial role of language and communication through which the actors of international trade acquire the information needed to coordinate and carry out international trade activities in reality.

In Sec. 1.1, we discuss conceptual and measurement issues of economic and societal prosperity, for both of which combined we propose to use the term "national wealth", quite deliberately in reference to the way the term has been used in the long tradition of Political Economy, from Smith, via Mill and Marx, to Coase in modern times. Section 1.2 will then provide an overview of the level and distribution of wealth in the world. Following this, we shall, in Sec. 1.3, identify those countries, especially in East and Southeast Asia, which have experienced rapid economic, and related social development. Section 1.4, describes the nature and determinants of industrialisation and economic development, with a particular focus on the role of international trade.

1.1 Concept and Measurement of National Wealth

This study assumes that increasing national wealth is a widely accepted social goal across countries of widely diverging cultural, political, and economic and physical conditions. By accepting national wealth as a goal, societies recognise the importance of material living conditions as a basis for the stability of and between societies, and the options and opportunities which these societies can offer to individuals, and may be a necessary condition for the survival of modern economies in an integrating world economy (see below, Sec. 1.3).

1.1.1 *National wealth*

The pursuit of national and individual wealth is the fundamental rationale of the economic activity of countries, organisations and individuals. To a large extent, the economic capacity of a society determines the well-being of its people and its standing in the international community. On an individual level, productivity and income determine to a large extent the options and choices open to and independently controlled by the individual. (Dahrendorf, 1979: *passim*)

Economic wealth, and the ways and means to achieve it, is also the classical subject of the discipline of economics, or, as it was initially called, the discipline of political economy. It is no accident that Adam Smith's *Inquiry into the Nature and the Causes of the Wealth of Nations* (1776) is seen as the foundation stone of political economy: the title of the work identifies the explanation of the determinants of economic prosperity as the subject of the new academic discipline.

Hence, a key issue for economists in relation to economic wealth has always been how to define and measure this wealth in a changing world. The question has lost none of its relevance.

1.1.2 *Measuring the level of economic activity*

Economists commonly use Gross Domestic Product (GDP), and GDP per capita, as the basic statistic to measure and compare levels of economic performance. GDP can be defined as a measure of all final goods and services produced in an economy by domestic factors of production in a given period of time (normally a year), valued at market prices. Derivatives of these statistics, the annual growth rate of GDP, and the annual growth rate of GDP per capita, are used to measure changes and development over time.

Normally, corrections of GDP to account for the effects of changes in the general price level will be made, in order to arrive at the quantity component of GDP, the so-called "real GDP". Often, Gross National Product (GNP) is used instead of GDP. The conceptual difference is that GDP counts the economic activities within an economy ("domestic"), whereas GNP counts the economic activities of the citizens of a country ("national"), regardless of where these activities take place. For the measurement of the wealth of a country, GDP is the more appropriate and the more intuitive measure, because it obviously relates more closely to the living conditions in a given country.

Growth rates of GDP are commonly used to trace economic growth over time. The concept of "economic growth", however, is much wider than that of GDP growth rates. Kuznets' modern definition identifies a country's economic growth as:

> "a long-term rise in capacity to supply increasingly diverse economic goods to its population, this growing capacity based on advancing technology and the institutional and ideological adjustments that it demands." (Kuznets, 1973)

All three prinicipal components of this definition are of great importance, as has been pointed out by Todaro, who also emphasises the social implications and individual adjustments which go hand in hand with economic growth:

> "The sustained rise in national output is a manifestation of economic growth, and the ability to provide a wide range of goods is a sign of economic maturity.
>
> Advancing technology provides the basis or preconditions for continuous economic growth — a necessary but not sufficient condition.

> To realize the potential for growth inherent in new technology, institutional, attitudinal, and ideological adjustments must be made. Technological innovation without concommitant social innovation is like a bulb without electricity — the potential exists, but without the complementary input, nothing will happen." (Todaro, 1994: 99)

The wide availability of GDP statistics for the majority of countries, and over comparatively long periods of time, often several decades, lends itself to an uncritical use of those statistics as direct measures of economic performance and economic growth, and as indicators of national wealth. Higher growth rates are uncritically interpreted and perceived as evidence of "better" performance, and policy makers sometimes seem to become obsessed with the aim of scoring higher growth rates of GDP, understood to be synonymous with increasing national wealth.

The first two Five-Year-Plans (1949–1953 and 1954–1958) and the "Great Leap Forward" of 1957/58 in the People's Republic of China, masterminded by Mao Zedong, provide an extreme, yet instructive example of misguided social and economic policies designed to generate economic growth. The period from 1949 to 1956 yielded high growth rates. This growth was achieved through an overemphasis on heavy industry and the production of investment goods. The material living conditions of the ordinary Chinese hardly improved in terms of supplying "increasingly diverse economic goods to its population". The "Great Leap Forward", which followed the abortion of the second Five-Year-Plan, certainly made ideological adjustments, but it was based on a misconception of technology, and failed accordingly.

Todaro, referring to this model critically — indeed in derogatory terms — as the "Growth Game", writes:

> "Economists and politicians from all nations, rich and poor, capitalist, socialist, and mixed, have worshipped at the shrine of economic growth. At the end of every year, statistics are compiled for all countries of the world showing their relative rates of GNP growth. 'Growthmanship' has become a way of life. Governments can rise or fall if their economic growth performance ranks high or low on this global scorecard." (Todaro 1994: 99)

1.1.3 *Social indicators of national wealth*

Even as a strict measure of economic activity, the limitations of GDP arising from its definition, and the problems occurring when estimating some of its components, are obvious. They are discussed in any intermediate and most introductory textbooks of macroeconomics. They include problems of:

- distinguishing between final and intermediate goods;
- distinguishing between domestic and foreign-owned factors of production;
- allocating the production of some goods to a specific period of time;
- determining the value of products with no prices, or no market prices;
- accounting equally for goods and services, regardless of their intrinsic value to society;
- the existence of an underground economy; and
- calculating an appropriated measure for deflating GDP at market prices.

There are also many who have pointed out the shortcomings of GDP as a broader indicator of economic well-being. The now almost dormant Quality-of-Life discussion, especially the so-called Social Indicators Movement, has produced valuable criticisms of these narrow economic concepts, and suggested a number of alternatives for growth accounting.

Early contributions to this discussions included the awareness-rising report of the Club of Rome (Meadows *et al.*, 1972), and influential policy papers (Gross, 1966; Toward a Social Report, 1970; Toward Balanced Growth, 1970; Juster, 1971). A dedicated academic journal, *Social Indicators Research — An International and Interdisciplinary Journal for Quality-of-Life Measurement*, was first published in May 1974 as a central clearing house for research dealing with descriptive, evaluative, and normative problems related to the measurement of the quality of life. The journal has published a steady stream of research, including many proposals for constructing and using measures other than GDP, some of which have had an impact. More recently, some serious attempts have been made to develop broader statistical measures, such as the Human Development Index (UNDP 1990), the "real wealth" measure proposed by the World Bank (1995), and the work of a group of economists in the United States called *Redefining Progress*, who are calling for "new measures of progress", such as the Genuine Progress Indicator (GPI). None of them is as yet an accepted substitute, nor an intended substitute for GDP or GDP per capita statistics.

Caution is also warranted when economic performance and economic growth are compared between different countries. Particularly in less developed countries, fewer economic activities are channelled through markets. Consequently, these countries have a relatively lower GDP than their more advanced counterparts.

It is worthwhile being aware of these limitations of the use of GDP and its statistical derivatives, especially when making international comparisons. It is not helpful however to invent, after twenty years of discussion, an "all too frequent presumption that the well-being of a community or nation improves because of a rise in GDP which is based on a statistic derived from the United Nations System of National Accounts," in order to subsequently ridicule its use as an indicator (Waring, 1988: 38). GDP is not a measure of, and does not cause, economic well-being or social welfare, but is an overall measure of the level of economic activity.

The beneficial impact of economic growth on society and the livelihood of any individual are plain to see. "Growth has transformed our world completely, and in the late twentieth century we have become accustomed to the idea of rates of growth which dramatically alter the prosperity of a nation during the lifetime of any individual." (Ormerod, 1994: 22). The benefits of growth are not simply a matter of increased material possessions. In reality, economic growth enables the production of more and better goods and services, with less labour input. In many ways, it is the increased leisure time that has had the most enriching and liberating impact on people, certainly in those countries that have experienced long periods of economic growth.

In the following sections, where we have attempted to identify groups of countries with different levels of economic prosperity, as well as with different speeds of development, the availability of data across a large number of countries was paramount. We have, therefore, relied mainly on conventional economic statistics, i.e. real GDP and real GDP per capita. Both are concise indicators, and the most commonly used measures of the productive performance of an economy. Indeed, there is not much wrong with the concept of GDP, as long as its definition and estimation, and the limitations to interpretation that arise from them, are observed. After all, few would doubt the usefulness of a car odometer engineered to measure distance traveled, even if it does not accurately reflect the more complex general wear and tear of a car.

But we have also looked at social indicators other than GDP per capita, and therefore, at broader concepts of measuring national wealth.

1.2 Comparing National Wealth Internationally

Towards the end of the twentieth century, two observations with regard to the national wealth of countries stand out. They are:

- an uneven yet stable distribution of economic performance across countries and
- a close relationship between economic performance and societal welfare

1.2.1 *The distribution of economic performance*

The first observation is that national wealth is very unevenly distributed across countries. The World Development Report, published annually since 1977 by the World Bank, regularly reports world development indicators, most recently in 1995, for 132 countries.

On the basis of GNP per capita for 1993, the report distinguishes four groups of economies: low-income economies with GNP per capita of $695 or less; lower-middle-income economies with GNP per capita of $696 to $2,800; upper-middle-income economies with GNP per capita of $2,801 to $8,625; and high-income economies with GNP per capita of $8,626 or more (World Bank, 1995: 157). The extent of economic inequality for 1993, as reflected by those indicators, is shown in Table 1.

Excluding China and India, the low-income group of economies with an average GNP per capita of $300 comprises 43 countries (out of a total of 132), most of them in Africa, and South and Southeast Asia. Their combined total GDP for 1993 was $340b, or 1.5 per cent of the world's total. There are 41 lower-middle-income economies, with an average GNP per capita of $1,590, and 22 upper-middle-income economies, with an average GNP per capita of $4,370. Their respective shares in the world's GDP was 7.3 and 9.4 per cent. The high-income group of economies comprises 22 countries. Their average income per capita is $23,090, and their combined GDP is $18,248b, or

Table 1. Selected Economic Statistics of National Wealth

	GNP per capita					
	Dollars 1993	Dollars 1988	% of 1993 avg.	% of 1988 avg.	Avg. growth 1980–1993	Assets
Low-income	380	320	8.6	9.2	3.7	20/20a
Excl China/India	300	280	6.8	8.1	0.1	–
Middle-income	2,480	1,930	56.1	55.6	0.2	–
lower-middle	1,590	1,380	36.0	39.8	–0.5	–
upper-middle	4,370	3,240	98.9	93.4	0.9	–
High-income	23,090	17,080	522.4	492.2	2.2	–
Total reporting	4,420	3,470	–	–	1.2	20/20b

Sources: World Bank (1990, 1995); Zagorin (1995).

Notes: (a) including Cambodia which is not included in the World Bank group of low-income coutries; (b) including Qatar, which is not included in the World Bank group of high-income economies.

79.0 per cent. This last group includes all of North America, all of Western Europe and Japan. Also included in this group are Hong Kong and Singapore.

A recent, exploratory study of the World Bank, reported by Zagorin (1995: 35), suggests a composite index of three dimensions of economic assets: produced assets, such as machinery, factories, roads and other productive infrastructure; natural assets, such as minerals, land, water and other natural resources; and human assets, employing criteria such as nutrition and educational levels. This index is different from GDP, in that the latter is restrict to income flows.

Column 6 of Table 1 shows how many of the top and bottom twenty countries, according to this new measure of economic wealth, also appear in the high- and low-income groups of economies, as measured by GDP per capita. The result is, that while there are some interesting reshuffles within groups of countries — for example, Australia and Canada, with their large land mass and low populations, emerge as the wealthiest countries — the top twenty countries are identical[1] on both lists, and all of the bottom twenty countries of the new study also appear in the group of low-income countries.

[1]See notes (a) and (b) in Table 1.

In addition to being distinct, the groups of countries with vastly different levels of economic wealth appear to also have a stable composition over time. In other words, the low-income economies seem to remain largely the same, as do the members of the other groups. It seems that there is little mobility between groups. Everyday usage of terms also confirms this impression: the distinction between the poor Less Developed Countries (LDCs) and the rich developed or industrialised countries is fairly clear, and is handled with instinctive certitude in classifying countries.

Table 1 contains, in columns 3 to 5, data which may give some clue as to why the groups are in general so stable. Average annual growth figures of GNP per capita 1980 – 1991 (Table 1, column 5) differ between the groups. In low-income economies, GNP per capita appears to have grown by a high average of 3.7 per cent between 1980 and 1993 — a rather high figure at first glance. This, however, is a deceptive figure, because it includes China and India, which, over the same period, experienced average annual economic growth of 7.8 and 3.2 per cent, respectively. Without the two "giants", the low-income economies achieved only an average of 0.1 per cent growth annually. In fact, 23 of the 45 economies in this group averaged negative growth rates over this thirteen-year period.

This did little to close the gap to the middle-income economies, although these averaged only 0.2 per cent growth themselves over the same period.

Interestingly, the lower-middle income group of countries fared even worse than the lowest group, with an average –0.5 per cent growth. The upper-middle income group appears to have been more successful, with a corresponding average growth rate of 0.9 per cent. This latter impression is, however, again deceptive. As in the case of the low-income countries, average economic growth is distorted by some high achievers: the countries of the East Asia and the Pacific, and of the South Asian region achieved average rates of 6.4 and 3.0 per cent, respectively, over the thirteen-year period. All other regions had actually negative growth rates. We shall return to this important finding in much more detail in Sec. 1.3.

In contrast to the low-income and middle-income economies, the high-income economies grew by an average of 2.2 per cent between 1980 and 1993.

This dynamic pattern — persistent low growth in low-income and middle-income countries, and sustained high growth in the high-income and two other sub-groups of countries — explains how it is that the composition of the groups does not change much. It goes further than that, and actually suggests that economic wealth in the world is becoming more and more unequal, making an escape from poverty all the more difficult, particularly for poorer countries.

If we relate average GNP per capita of the low income economies to that of the high-income economies for the years of 1988 and 1993 (Table 1, columns 3 and 4), we find further support for this hypothesis. In 1988, average GNP per capita in the low-income economies, excluding China and India, was 8.1 per cent of the world's average of $4,420. Within the following five years, this fell to 6.8 per cent, making these economies relatively poorer. This relative fall is also true, although to a lesser extent, for the lower middle-income countries. Their relative level of GNP per capita fell from 39.8 to 36.0 per cent. By contrast, the high-income economies improved their relative standing, from 492.2 in 1988, to 522.4 per cent of the world's average in 1993. This improvement is also true for the upper middle-income economies as a whole, but again, the East Asian and Pacific economies may have distorted the finding. They improved their relative income position from 15.6 to 18.6 per cent of the world's average.

The conclusion is quite unambiguous. Indeed, as far as economic wealth is concerned, there are distinct groups of countries, the composition of which is stable. In addition, the boundaries between groups of different economic wealth are hard to overcome, especially since 1988.

With this background, it seems even more important to study those factors that have enabled some countries to succeed against the odds. These countries are to be found in Asia, especially in East and Southeast Asia. Before we turn to them specifically, we shall now look into the social dimension of national wealth.

1.2.2 *The social dimension of national wealth*

The first observation in our comparison of international wealth in the previous section concerned the distribution of economic performances. The second observation is that the admittedly debatable social indicators and indices of national wealth suggest that economic prosperity and general well-being tend to coincide, even though the former is only one aspect of the latter. Table 2 shows a selection of two conventional social indicators, and one modern composite

Table 2. Selected Social Indicators of National Wealth

	Life Expectancy at Birth [years]	Adult Illiteracy [%]	Human Development Index 1990			
			low	medium	high	very high
Low-income	62	41	82.2	17.8	–	
Excl China/India	56	49				
Middle-income	68	17	11.9	50.8	35.6	1.7
lower-middle	67	19	17.9	56.4	25.6	–
upper-middle	69	14	–	40	55.0	5.0
High-income	77	4	–	–		
Total reporting	66	33	–	4.2	8.3	87.5

Sources: World Bank (1995); UNDP (1990)

index, the Human Development Index. Here, because we are interested mostly in the relationship between economic performance and societal welfare, we have repeated the pattern of income groups introduced in Table 1 in the previous section.

Two important social indicators in Table 2, life expectancy at birth and adult illiteracy, relate directly to health and education. By selecting these two statistics in addition to the conventional economic statistic of GDP per capita, we follow a view that has been consistent over the last decades of social indicators research, specifically that:

> "at all levels of development, the three essential [choices] are for people to lead a long and healthy life, to acquire knowledge and to have access to resources needed for a decent standard of living." (UNDP, 1990: 10)

Furthermore, we use the Human Development Index (HDI), which is based on three basic indicators — life expectancy, literacy and (the log of) real GDP[2]

[2]The logarithm reflects that there are diminishing returns in the conversion of additional income into the fulfilment of needs.

per capita.[3] The HDI may seem conceptually redundant, but the way in which it combines human development in one statistic, and normalises it by comparing it to the highest achiever, is distinct from looking at the three indicators separately.

The statistics in Table 2 show a high correlation of the social indicators with income per capita, at least on the level of the four groups of countries. Life expectancy at birth is lowest (56 years) in low-income economies (excluding China and India), somewhat higher (67 and 69 years) in middle-income economies, and significantly higher (77 years) in high-income economies. Similarly, but of course negatively correlated, adult illiteracy is highest (49%) in low-income economies, lower (19 and 14%) in middle-income economies, and only 4% in high-income economies.

A similar picture emerges from the HDI. The correlation of the HDI with GNP per capita appears to be strong. 82.2 per cent of countries which belong to the low-income group are also those countries with the lowest human development, as measured by an HDI value of less than 50% of the highest value (Japan). If one takes into account that six of the remaining nine countries are just outside the numerical limit for what constitutes "low" human development in the Human Development Report, the relationship appears even closer.

For middle-income countries, the evidence of a close relationship between income and human development appears to be less clear. Table 2 shows that 50.8 per cent of them belong to the corresponding medium human development group. By comparison, 35.6 per cent of the middle-income countries belong to the high human development category. The UNDP report infers from this that country-by-country data "reveal that the disparity among countries is much greater in income than in human development." (UNDP, 1990: 15) This is correct, but it is only a logical consequence of using the log of GNP per capita, which obviously reduces the weight of income in the HDI, and of an arbitrary cut-off point of what constitutes "high" human development. The UNDP report puts the cut-off point between medium and high human development at HDI = 0.8, i.e. 80 per cent of the highest mark achieved by any country (Japan = 1.0). As a result, the countries in the high human development group number 55, and correspondingly, many of the middle-income countries appear

---

[3]A mathematical formulation of the HDI is contained in Technical Note 3 of the Human Development Report 1990 (UNDP 1990: 109).

in the high human development group. A more cautious interpretation would be to say that the differences in income are likely to overstate the differences in living conditions, especially in upper middle-income countries.

A very close relationship between income level and human development is clearly evident again among the high-income countries. All but three of them are also in the group of very high human development, defined by at least 90% of the highest developed country. Or, to put it differently, 21 of the 24 highest income economies are also among the 24 highest developed countries, as measured by the HDI. Of the remaining three countries, two are special cases, Kuwait and the United Arab Emirates, oil-rich countries whose GNP per capita is deceptively high, thus obscuring an otherwise lower level of human development. The third country is Singapore, one of those countries we shall return to in the next section.

1.3 High-Performing Asian Economies 1960–1995

So far, by comparing levels of national wealth, we have confirmed first the uneven yet stable distribution of national wealth, and, second, the close relationship between its two components, economic and social wealth.

One of these points — that of stability of income groups over time — may obscure an important third observation, which has been hinted at already. This third observation is that, while the four large groups of economies seem to change little over time, there are notable exceptions to the general stability of this pattern of low-, middle-, and high-income countries, in that some countries and sub-groups of countries have been exceptionally successful. Because this study relates specifically to two of them, we turn our attention now to them.

A closer look at regional groupings of economies reveals that East Asia, comprising all the 23 low- and middle-income economies of East, Southeast Asia and the Pacific, east of and including China and Thailand, have had a remarkable record of high and sustained economic growth from 1965 to 1990 (see Fig. 1, World Bank, 1993a: 2).

Figure 1 shows an average annual growth rate of 5.3 per cent for East Asia over a quarter of a century, from 1965 to 1990. Most of this achievement can be attributed to the performance of a subset of eight economies, for which the World Bank uses the term High-Performing Asian Economies (HPAE).

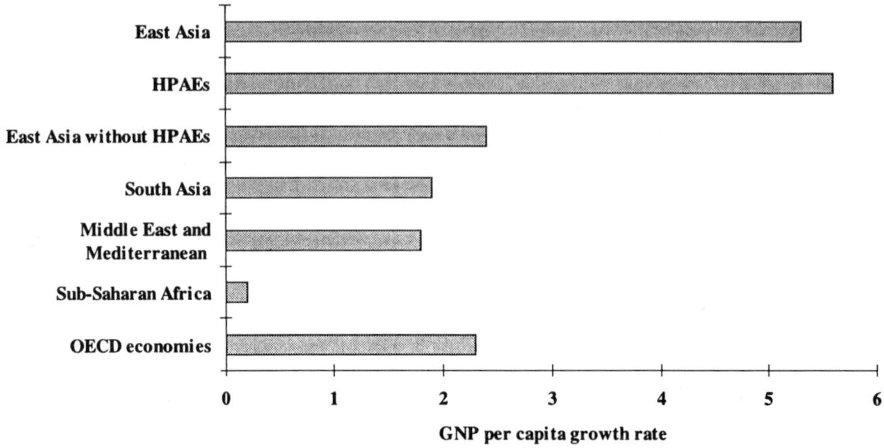

Fig. 1 Average Economic Growth of GNP per capita, 1965–90.

The HPAEs at present include:

- Japan,
- the Four Tigers: Hong Kong, the Republic of Korea, Singapore, and Taiwan (China), and
- the Newly Industrialising Economies: Indonesia, Malaysia, and Thailand.

The economic performance of the HPAEs is very remarkable. They achieved an average annual growth rate of GNP per capita of 5.6 per cent over a period of 25 years, thereby almost quadrupling incomes. This achievement is about twice as good as that of most other regional groups of countries, which achieved an average of a roughly two per cent annual growth, equivalent to a 1.6-fold increase in income over 25 years. The Four Tigers and Indonesia had the highest growth rates of GNP per capita of all countries in the world, with the exception of Botswana, which occupies first spot.

In terms of the groups of countries discussed in the last section, Japan is ranked second among high-income economies. The Four Tigers have been growing for several decades, and have joined (in the case of Hong Kong and Singapore) or have approached (in the case of Korea and Taiwan) the ranks of high income countries. The Newly Industrialising Economies (Indonesia, Malaysia and Thailand) are fast moving upwards.

As we have seen before, economic growth appears to go hand in hand with a general improvement of national wealth. This has also been true for the HPAEs:

> "As a result of rapid, shared growth, human welfare has improved dramatically. Life expectancy in the developing HPAEs increased from 56 years in 1960 to 71 years in 1990. (In other low- and middle-income economies, life expectancy also rose considerably, from 36 and 49 to 62 and 66 years, respectively.) In the HPAEs, the proportion of people living in absolute poverty, lacking such basic necessities as clean water, food, and shelter, dropped — for example, from 58 per cent in 1960 to 17 per cent in 1990 in Indonesia, and from 37 per cent to less than 5 per cent in Malaysia during the same period. (...) A host of other social and economic indicators, from education to appliance ownership, have also improved rapidly in the HPAEs and now are at levels that sometimes surpass those in industrial economies." (World Bank, 1993: 4)

A recent report by the Economic Planning Agency of the Government of Japan (*White Paper on the World Economy*, 1994, *passim*) confirms that the HPAEs have continued to grow into the mid-1990s. (See also *Asia Yearbook* 1994). Table 3 shows recent annual growth rates for the HPAEs, i.e. for the Four Tigers, the Southeast Asian NIEs, including a fourth ASEAN member, the Philippines, China, and Vietnam.

Table 3 shows that the Four Tigers and the NIEs continued to experience strong economic growth. Growth rates for these seven HPAEs (excluding Japan), for the four years up to and including 1994 (first six months only), range from 5.1 (Hong Kong, 1991; Korea, 1992) to 11.3 per cent (Singapore, 1994, 1st quarter) and are on an average far higher than the 1965 to 1990 average of 5.6 per cent reported in Fig. 1. It also appears that the economic stagnation on the Philippines, not included normally in the HPAEs, has been overcome. The Economic Planning Agency notes that while exports to industrialised countries are still important, the growth process now has more internal strength, with those exports being backed up by strong domestic consumption demand, investment demand for plant and equipment, investment demand for social

Table 3. Asian Economies: Growth Performance 1991 to 1994

				1994	
	1991	1992	1993	1–3	4–6
Four Tigers	7.4	5.5	5.7	–	–
Korea	9.1	5.1	5.5	9.2	7.9
Taiwan (China)	7.2	6.0	5.9	5.6	5.8
Hong Kong	5.1	6.0	5.9	5.7	5.4
Singapore	6.7	6.0	9.9	11.8	9.3
Southeast Asian NIEs	6.4	6.1	6.4	–	–
Indonesia	6.9	6.4	6.5	6.9	7.1
Thailand	8.1	7.6	7.8	–	–
Philippines	–0.5	0.1	2.0	3.7	4.5
Malaysia	8.7	7.8	8.5	8.8	–
China	8.0	13.2	13.4	11.4a	–
Vietnam	6.0	7.5	8.0	–	–

Note: (a) For January to September 1994.
Source: White Paper on the World Economy1994: 9

infrastructure and rapid increases in intra-regional trade. Table 3 also shows the strong economic performance of China and Vietnam.

These statistics, together covering almost 35 years, are unambiguous and impressive. In fact, the economic transformation is such that the typical incrementalism of economic and social change, which applies to most other societies, may not apply in the HPAEs. For those who had the good fortune of living in any of the HPAEs for any significant period of time over the last decades, personal experience of the dynamism, the optimism, and perhaps the boldness of economic development and change as part of everyday life, has probably been left with a much more lasting impression than statistical data may suggest to the distant analyst. Within short time spans indeed, the appearance and very substance of cities and people's livelihood have changed and continue to change dramatically in these societies, and nowhere more visibly so than in Hong Kong and Macau.

Quite understandably, this achievement has attracted popular interest the world over. The familiarity of terms like "Asian Economic Miracle" and the "Pacific Century" owes much to this economic achievement. It has also attracted the attention of policy makers, keen to learn what may be learnt from the model. Indeed, within East Asia, and the group of HPAEs themselves, there may be a leader-follower pattern. Japan certainly was the first economy leading the emergence of East Asia as an economic force. The Four Tigers followed from the mid-1960s, with the Newly Industrialising Economies in pursuit since the early eighties. Chen (1979: *passim*), referring to the characteristic image of migrating birds in flight, used "Flying Geese" as a metaphor for the progress of Asian nations in the world. Chen has since given up referring to the "Flying Geese", mostly a reflection of research, which has shown remarkable differences between the different countries. But policy makers, international organisations and researchers continue to emphasise common threads among the HPAEs, which may still hold important policy and strategy lessons for others. Since 1979, China has been trying to join with *Deng Xiaoping*'s stated objective "to create many Hong Kongs," indicating, again, the idea of the leader-follower pattern. And most recently, Vietnam has embarked on a similar path with the *doi moi* policy of economic renovation and liberalisation.

The World Bank, in its Policy Research Report "The East Asian Miracle" (World Bank, 1993a), comes to the conclusion that there has been, and still is, a successful "model", one that, at least for a significant number of countries and under present conditions, seems to work. Specifically, sustained economic growth seems to go hand in hand with a number of factors:

- flexibility;
- emphasis on education;
- market orientation and
- internationalisation.

Flexibility refers to the preparedness of society for the rapid change of the economic structure, the social fabric, and the ideological beliefs, and the political and institutional adjustments that is perhaps a prerequisite, but is certainly conducive to sustained economic growth. Emphasis on education means the willingness and ability to provide the funding and political support necessary to develop the quantity and quality of human resources that make a modern economy possible. Market orientation requires the political will to reduce the direct involvement of the government in the economy, and instead to allow for a large private sector in the economy to operate without government intervention and to introduce predictable and reinforcible rules and regulations. Finally, closely related to the preparedness for change is the orientation towards internationalisation of the economy, i.e. the propensity to develop and expand the foreign economic relations of the economy with the rest of the world, and with it, to accept mutual dependency.

Our interest is a better understanding of those factors that appear to have played a major and positive role in the ability of the HPAEs to achieve a high level of national wealth within the last few decades.

1.4 The Wealth — Trade Link

The World Bank term of High-Performing Asian Economies refers to the level of economic performance of certain economies, in relation to others. In the context of taking stock of the national wealth of different countries, this is appropriate. However, turning our attention to those factors that have caused high performance, a dynamic perspective is required.

1.4.1 *Trade, industrialisation and economic development*

This discussion has been conducted in the modern literature under the heading Newly Industrialising Countries (NICs), or, synonymously, Newly Industrialising Economies (NIEs). The OECD adopted in 1979 three general criteria for categorising a developing country as a NIE (Grimwade, 1989: 312):

- Fast growth in both the absolute level of industrial employment and the share of industrial employment in total employment.
- A rising share of world exports in manufactures.
- Fast growth in real per capita GDP such that the country was successful in narrowing the gap with the advanced industrialised countries.

According to this definition, the term NIE denotes a transitory Mand dynamic phase of the economic development of a country, characterised by (rapid) industrialisation and therefore high performance.

It has been argued that Japan was the first NIE. This, however, overlooks the fact that the early stages of Japan's economic take-off were peculiar to the post-war situation (Tsuru, 1993). In particular, export growth was not the main driving force in those early stages. Up to the end of the 1980s, the Four Tigers — Hong Kong, Korea, Singapore, and Taiwan (China) — were normally referred to as NIEs, in the sense of the above definition. (see James, Naya and Meier, 1987: 1–3). The Four Tigers are perceived as having gone through the phase of "new" industrialisation, and are "well on their way to joining the club of developed industrial countries." (Haberler, 1988: 4). The term is now used, for example, in the most recent World Development Report (World Bank, 1995) for Indonesia, Malaysia and Thailand. Officially since the end of 1978, but on any significant scale only since the early 1980s, China has been liberalising its economy, initially its foreign sector (trade, foreign direct investment, exchange rate devaluation). As a result, increased imports and foreign capital inflows have been inducing further domestic restructuring. In Vietnam and India, similar outward-looking policies have been instigated since the late 1980s.

Indeed, there is no doubt that high economic performance is the beneficial and desired outcome of industrialisation, and has been ever since the industrial revolution. The real question is not how an economy can be industrialised, but how an industrial structure can be achieved, that allows for the sustainable, strong economic growth that Kuznets had in mind. For evidence of industrialisation that has not performed this important task, one need look no further back than the experience of the People's Republic of China between 1949 and 1978. China had one of the highest industrialisation rates in the world, but failed thoroughly in achieving a competitive, high-performing economy.

The question of how to achieve an efficient industrial structure conducive to sustainable, strong economic growth was the central topic of the World Development Report 1987. It concluded that "this quest for efficient industrialisation relates directly to foreign trade." (Rajapatirana, 1987: 2) This view is also shared by Haberler (1988: 5):

> "Experience of the past thirty years or so has clearly shown that development policies that pay little attention to the vital contribution of foreign trade, private enterprise, and direct foreign investment, do not yield sustained and efficient industrialisation and growth."

The first effect of international trade is a static effect. This effect of international trade is a direct and logical extension of the theory of specialisation and exchange. Already in *The Wealth of Nations*, these theoretical cornerstones are to be found in the famous opening paragraphs, of the first and second chapters respectively, of the first book.

Chapter I, headed *Of the Division of Labour*, begins:

> "The great improvements in the productive powers of Labour, and the greater part of the skill, dexterity and judgment with which it is any where directed, or applied, seem to have been the effects of the division of labour." (Smith, 1776: 5)

Chapter II, headed *Of the Principle which gives Occasion to the Division of Labour*, begins as if seamlessly connected:

> "This division of labour, from which so many advantages are derived, is not originally the effect of any human wisdom, which foresees and intends that general opulence to which it gives occasion. It is the necessary, though very slow and gradual consequence of a certain propensity in human nature which has in view no such extensive utility; the propensity to truck, barter, and exchange one thing for another." (Smith, 1776: 16)

In obvious analogy, the gains from international trade and the international division of labour enable countries to specialise and to export those things that they can produce more cheaply in exchange for what others can provide at lower cost. The advantage of international trade to a country is a more efficient employment of its productive forces. Foreign trade is, as John St. Mill put it, "virtually a mode of cheapening production; and in all such cases the consumer is the person (who) ultimately benefited." (Mill 1848: 118) This has been and still is one of the basic factors promoting economic well-being and increasing national income for all countries involved.

The static effect from trade assumes no change of the productive capabilities to result from trade. This would imply an unchanged production possibilities boundary, with the effect being limited to a choice of product combinations.

The second effect, or rather the secondary effects, of international trade are indirect, and relate to the changes in the productive structure of an economy which international trade induces and promotes. These are the effects from trade, which make possible the development of an efficient industrial structure, which we earlier identified as crucial for high and sustained economic growth.

It would seem that there are chiefly four indirect, or dynamic effects. These effects are:

- Provision of material means (capital goods, machinery, raw and semifinished materials) indispensable for economic development.
- Dissemination of technological knowledge, transmission of ideas, importation of know-how, skills, managerial talents and entrepreneurship.
- Availability of capital in the form of loans, share holdings, and direct foreign investment.
- Maintenance of a healthy degree of competition subjecting domestic producers to international product and production process standards.

It may be worthwhile to quote a longer, classical passage of the *Principles of Political Economy*, which not only contains the factors just named, but expresses the wide economic and social implications of international trade on countries. Referring to the static effects of foreign trade, Mill writes (1848: 118–119):

> "But there are, besides, indirect effects, which must be counted as benefits of a high order. One is, the tendency of every extension of the market to improve the process of production. A country which produces for a larger market than its own, can introduce a more extended division of labour, can make greater use of machinery, and is more likely to make inventions and improvements in the process of production. Whatever causes a greater quantity of anything to be produced in the same place, tends to the general increase of productive powers of the world. There is another consideration, principally applicable to an early stage of industrial advancement. A people may be in a quiescent, indolent, uncultivated state, with few wants and wishes, all their tastes being either fully satisfied or entirely undeveloped, and they may fail to put forth the whole of their productive energies for want of any sufficient object of desire. The opening of foreign trade, by making them acquainted with new objects, or tempting them by the easier acquisition of things which they had not previously thought

> attainable, sometimes works a complete industrial revolution in a country whose resources were previously undeveloped for want of energy and ambition in the people. (...)"
>
> But the economical advantages of commerce are surpassed in importance by those of its effects which are intellectual and moral. It is hardly possible to overrate the value, for the improvement of human beings, of things which bring them into contact with persons dissimilar to themselves, and with modes of thought and action unlike those with which they are familiar. (...) Commercè is the purpose of the far greater part of the communication which takes place between civilised nations. Such communication has always been, and is peculiarly in the present age, one of the primary sources of progress."[4]

We may safely conclude that the positive and close link between international trade, industrialisation and national wealth is not in any doubt, as far as causality is concerned. And, of course, Mill's explicit reference to the central role of the communication that accompanies trade, will be of major interest further down.

In the final section of this first chapter, we shall briefly review the actual globalisation of economic activity, which, independent of theoretical thought, establishes international trade as a key feature of the modern world economy.

1.4.2 *International trade and production: The global economy*

International trade has long been a feature of economic activity. But it has not dominated economic activity until quite recently. One only needs to look into any introductory economics textbook to see that, until recently, international trade and a number of related topics were additions to the mainstream treatment of the domestic economy and typically added at the end of the book, virtually as miscellanea.

---

[4]The omitted sentences in the middle of the second paragraph, as well as what follows, relate to the positive influence which foreign trade may have on peace between countries. Mill's views sound naive and overly optimistic on that score.

This has fundamentally changed over the last two decades, which have seen economic integration on a world scale. This economic integration makes itself felt mostly through international trade and international capital flows.

By 1990, the volume of goods and services traded across borders accounted for 45 per cent of world GDP, up from 25 per cent in 1970. About one in five jobs worldwide depends directly or indirectly on trade (World Bank, 1995: 51).

Similarly, capital flows have almost doubled, especially foreign direct investment. In the case of Japan, the transmission mechanism from export trade to subcontracting relationships and strategic international partnerships, then on to direct foreign investment, is particularly impressive, although certainly not (yet) typical. Table 4 shows five-year averages of applications for direct foreign investment projects, as recorded by the Japanese Ministry of Finance.

The data in Table 4 show the enormous increase of direct foreign investment activities of Japanese companies. It appears that on the basis of five-year averages, direct foreign investment has virtually doubled every five years.

Table 4. Five-Year Averages of Japan's Direct Foreign Investment

Period	US$ billion
1956–60	0.09
1961–65	0.13
1966–70	0.53
1971–75	2.47
1976–80	4.13
1981–85	9.43
1986	22.32

Source: Tsuru (1993: 192)

The obvious conclusion derived from this international integration process, for which we have only provided selected illustrative evidence, is that international trade and the related international division of labour are the most significant economic forces driving and shaping the world economy. The lives of people around the world are increasingly connected through international trade, capital flows, and also labour migration. The complexity and utmost importance of these changes, and the economic, social and political impact that they have, would have been unthinkable just ten or twenty years ago. And the forces and conditions which they depend on are not sufficiently understood.

One of the primary sources of these developments, highlighted already by classical economists like Smith, and especially Mill, is the ability of people to communicate effectively and efficiently across cultural and linguistic barriers.

This monograph is written precisely on this topic. In the next chapter, we shall describe in detail the societies and economies of Hong Kong and Macau. There are arguably no better examples of high-performing trading economies, which so totally depend on multilingualism and communicative competencies for their living.

Chapter 2

The Industrial Organisation of International Trade: The Case of Hong Kong and Macau

Few societies could be said to be built on trade from their earliest days. For Hong Kong and Macau, trade has been the *raison d'être* and the lifeblood of their citizens over centuries. Their rises to periodic prosperity in the past, and in modern times their joint development "into one of the most prosperous and cosmopolitan cities in the world, standing in the top rank of international trading and financial centres" (MFAT 1995), make them most interesting, and because of their successful economic development, important societies to study. As far as the specific industry of textiles and garments is concerned, Hong Kong is today a world centre of fashion and design. There is no denying that a mere quarter of a century ago, Hong Kong in particular, along with Macau and much of Asia, were viewed in Europe (by those who knew of their existence and location) as seedy, third-world places. Even today, the reality of the thriving societies in Asia is far ahead of popular perception in Western countries.

The question is: How do they do it? One answer, hitherto largely disregarded, and explored in this study is — by their development and use of effective communication in an international language, transmitted very rapidly.

2.1 An Organisational Theory Perspective

As far as economic systems, for example private businesses, are concerned, this question is an entirely conventional one: it is concerned with the problems of designing organisations, and of the ways of managing these organisations efficiently. However, we use the term organisational design in a much broader sense. Specifically, we apply in Chapter 2 the concept of organisational design to entire economies and their constituent components, in our case, of the trading economies of Hong Kong and Macau.

While it may appear somewhat unusual to apply the concept of organisational design in this context, this perspective is indeed useful, because it recognises that an economic system evolves, and is often more or less deliberately designed to perform certain tasks well. For example, the economic system reform in the People's Republic of China post-1978 is primarily designed to achieve high economic growth, rather than an equitable distribution of income, which was the main goal of the pre-1978 system. The new design involves different institutions, different competencies, different coordination mechanisms, and different incentive systems. In the case of Hong Kong and Macau, their economies are particularly well designed to be successful trading economies.

A comprehensive organisation forms an entity, within and through which people and lower-level organisations interact and achieve individual and collective goals. An economy can be seen as such a comprehensive organisation, which consists of a network of people and organisations, with lower-level organisations linked together through higher-level organisations (Milgrom and Roberts, 1992: 19). This network enables people and organisations to cooperate. The different elements of an economy — individuals, businesses, government — can be studied separately, but they only work in conjunction.

Some economists have argued that this economic interacting and achieving is natural to human beings. Frank Knight (1941) writes: "[People] in general, and within limits, wish to behave economically, to make their activities and their organisations 'efficient' rather than wasteful." Gary S Becker's work[1] on the economics of a whole range of activities, including crime and marriage, would

[1] A concise overview of Gary S Becker's work, written in the context of his receiving the 1992 Nobel Prize in Economics, is to be found in Fuchs (1994: 183–192), notably in Table 1 (ibidem: 185).

also seem to support this assumption. And while some might have reservations about how far economic rationality determines people's behaviour and decision-making, only very few would doubt that organisations are conducive to, and tend to re-inforce, purposeful interaction and performance towards a collective, organisational goal.

An economic system consists of several, interconnected components. In principle, these are:

- the economic system as a whole,
- private and public organisations, and
- individual transactions.

The highest-level organisation is the economy as a whole. The foundations and fundamental "design concepts" on which Hong Kong and Macau are based and function, are outlined in Sec. 2.2. Obviously, this is first and foremost a topic which belongs to economic history and to the theory of macroeconomic institutions and policies. We shall outline only some essential features.

Those organisational entities, which correspond best to the popular concept of organisation, constitute the next lower level. They are the private and public enterprises, which comprise an industrial sector. They are also the semi-public and public organisations such as trade unions and government agencies. A key feature of these organisations, and one that is particularly relevant in business and trade, is that they possess legal identity. This enables them to enter contracts as organisations and in their own name, regardless of the individuals who belong to them. The structure of the textile and garment industry in Hong Kong and Macau, and characteristics of their businesses, are discussed in Sec. 2.3.

The most fundamental unit of analysis in organisation theory is the transaction — the transfer of goods and services from one owner to another. The ultimate participants in transactions are individual human beings. Their interests, behaviour and actions, the things they know and the things they do, are of equal fundamental importance for the understanding of how organisations work with regard to, say, macroeconomic policies and business finance. It is people — not economies nor enterprises — who actually decide and act. To use again Adam Smith's (1776: 5) words, their "skill, dexterity, and judgment with which [the productive power of labour] is anywhere directed" is crucial to the efficiency of the organisation, in this case the economies of Hong Kong and Macau. We shall discuss the nature and structure of transactions of international trade business, and the people who manage them, in Sec. 2.4.

In Sec. 2.5 of this chapter, we shall summarise the implications of the industrial organisation's perspective on international trade for the study of trade transactions and the communication flows on which they depend.

2.2 Trading Economies: The Macro-level

Section 2.2 presents a brief historical review of Hong Kong and Macau as trading places, and an update on the institutional and macro-economic policy framework — the "organisational design on the highest level" — of their contemporary economies.

2.2.1 *Cities as entrepots*

The unquestionable reason for the founding and continued existence of both Hong Kong and Macau up to the present is the function of *entrepot*, or marketplace, located at the South China coast, where goods and services into and out of China have been traded ever since international maritime trade began.

Of course, Macau is not only older than Hong Kong, but in the history of China's trade, and more broadly speaking, in enabling "the West to maintain continuous relations with China from 1557 onwards, [Macau is the more important]." (Coates, 1966: xi)

The foundation of Macau in the sixteenth century was the result of the Portuguese search for a permanent foothold for Portuguese sea-traders on the Chinese coast, in order to take advantage of the isolationist policies of China (Pires, 1991: 8; Cremer, 1991: 25). A location on the eastern side of the Pearl River Delta on the South China coast, about 150 km south of Guangzhou (Canton), and 50 km west of Hong Kong, across the estuary, was ideally suited to this purpose. This location was used at the time by Fujianese fishermen who maintained a Buddhist temple dedicated to the Goddess *A-Ma* at the tip of the peninsula. The fishermen called the natural port *A-Ma-Gao* (Port of *A-Ma*), which is the most generally accepted explanation for the name of Macau.

For almost a century, from 1554 to 1642, Macau became a trading centre on the main sea route from Europe to Japan, and entirely controlled the China–Japan trade (Coates, 1966: 3) The first link in this trade chain was the voyage between Portugal and India. The ships usually left Lisbon in March to arrive in Goa in September. Leaving Goa, where cotton textiles were loaded, in September, the ships sailed to Malacca and the Spice Islands. There, some of the fabrics were exchanged for spices, mainly pepper. The cargo of spices from the islands, cotton fabrics from India, metalware, cut glass, mirrors, clocks and wine from Europe, and jewellery from the Middle East, arrived in Macau in May. There, the cargo was exchanged against Chinese products, including porcelain, metals, and especially, Chinese silk. The Chinese silk, in particular, was in high demand in Japan, which paid in silver (Coates, 1978; Boxer, 1959).

As a result of this profitable trading business, Macau became the place in the Far East, "whence the riches of the neighbouring empire found their way to foreign countries" (Montalto de Jesus, 1926). At first, Macau appears to have had only a seasonal existence. The captain-general of the annual fleet, appointed by the Portuguese Crown, not only had the right to the profits derived from the journey, but also acted as interim governor of Macau. Growing rich, Macau also developed and matured politically. In 1576, the diocese of Macau was founded, including China, Japan and Korea. Macau became a bishop's seat in 1581. Spence (1985) provides a vivid description of the extent to which trade supported all aspects of life in Macau, including the controversial involvement of the Jesuits in the trade business. In 1585, the Senate was established, followed in 1586 by the privileges of a Portuguese city. Macau's population also grew quickly. Within twelve years of the arrival of the Portuguese, "a very large settlement on the point of the mainland, which is called Macau, with three churches and a hospital for the poor and house of Santa Misericordia" had been built (Boxer, 1965).

Macau's early success did not last. The Ming Dynasty, which the Portuguese had supported with arms trade, fell slowly apart. The Japanese closed their ports to the Portuguese traders and missionaries for religious reasons. And the Dutch took the Portuguese port of Malacca on the Malayan peninsula, cutting Macau off from the Manila-Mexico trade, and hence the trade across the Pacific. Trade and prosperity resumed for a short while after 1717, when the Qing government in Beijing closed all Chinese ports to foreign trade, allowing the Portuguese to resume their role as middlemen and traders.

The periodic rise and decline of Macau's prosperity are evidence of the close relationship between international trade and the national wealth of Macau: Macau was wealthy in the broadest sense of the word as long as trade flourished. When the latter faded, so did the city.

Since the beginning of the nineteenth century, China trade was carried out through foreign "factories" in Guangzhou. But trade was confined to the months of October through to May. Macau was still an important base for European traders in the off-season, despite the inconvenience of not having adequate port facilities, and it was also an important social centre for them and their families. This is, of course, well documented, and has also been the subject of a large number of historical novels (e.g. Clavell, 1966; Mo, 1986), which have helped create and extend an image of nineteenth century trading ports on the China coast in the West. The opium wars, related to Britain's demand for silver to pay for imports, led to increasing conflicts between China and Britain. Macau's reluctance to get involved in the conflict, and the fact that it did not have a harbour suitable for a new generation of ships with more draught, meant that the British were in need of a different maritime base. They found this base in Hong Kong, which China was forced to surrender to Britain in the Treaty of Nanjing in 1842. By the middle of the nineteenth century, Macau's function as a European base for China trade had shifted to Hong Kong.

Hong Kong grew fast. By 1859, its population was nearly 880,000, far bigger than Macau had ever been. At the turn of the century, Hong Kong handled 40 per cent of all of China's trade, on which its modest prosperity continued to depend throughout the first half of the twentieth century.

2.2.2 *Modern Hong Kong and Macau: From entrepot to industrial society*

As we have seen in the previous section, Hong Kong took over from Macau, and expanded the entrepot function about one-and-a-half centuries ago. But Hong Kong not only superseded Macau: it absorbed Macau's economy in the process. From an economic and social point of view, though not from a cultural, historical, and political one, post-1842 Macau is most appropriately seen and analysed as part of Hong Kong.

As an entrepot for nearly one hundred years, Hong Kong lived on trade and trade-related services. The legacy of this period included:

- the development of excellent port facilities,
- well-established shipping and trade links with other parts of the world,
- enterprises and staff experienced in international trade, and
- extensive personal connections overseas, particularly in South East Asia and the Pacific Rim.

All of these legacies proved to be valuable assets for Hong Kong in its post-war rise. In the years following the war, Hong Kong underwent reconstruction. The basic nature and pattern of the entrepot trade was resumed. The reconstruction was successful and generated annual growth rates of 35 per cent between 1947 and 1951. At the height of the Korean boom in 1951, Hong Kong's total exports stood at HK$4,433 million, higher than in 1962. But domestic exports, i.e. exports of goods produced in Hong Kong, were estimated at only HK$ 550 million. This implies that 87 per cent of Hong Kong's exports were actually re-exports (Lin and Lin, 1979: 226). Two thirds of its re-exports were to Southeast Asian markets.

The reconstructed entrepot economy, however, was short-lived. Tensions between China and the United States over Korea, and the establishment of the Communist government in China in 1949, led to a trade embargo on China in 1951. As a result, exports of Western machinery and industrial raw materials into China dwindled, as did Western demand for consumer goods from China. These events drastically reduced Hong Kong's entrepot business. In 1951–52, the share of re-exports to China as a percentage of total Hong Kong exports fell by half, from 36 to 18 per cent. However, the same political process which eroded the entrepot function brought with it entrepreneurial talent and capital from the mainland of China, and a large influx of immigrant workers. These were the seeds of new trade opportunities based on light industrial manufacture, predominantly of textiles and garments — not on entrepot trade.

From 1954 onwards, Hong Kong went through a rapid period of industrialisation. "Emigrant entrepreneurs" (Wong, 1988) from China, especially from Shanghai, reestablished themselves in Hong Kong, using their industrial skills and their financial and productive capital, which they had brought with them from China. They also used the international family networks and market connections, which had been built up over long periods. Simultaneously, the influx of unskilled workers provided the growing industrial economy with a steady, low-wage supply of labour: Between 1950 and 1980, the population of Hong Kong grew by approximately one million per decade, from two million in 1950 to five million in 1980.

The major industries in the industrialisation process were the textile and garment industries (see Table 5).

The time period for Table 5 has been chosen for a reason. As discussed above, Hong Kong had functioned well as an entrepot for the first century of its existence, and had also made a good start after the war in resuming this role. But the political changes of 1951–52 had all but eliminated the old model. In the period that followed, Hong Kong employed a new model of trade-oriented development. This new development model, by the middle of the 1980s, had taken Hong Kong nearly to the top of the middle-income countries in the world, roughly on a par with countries like New Zealand, Spain and Ireland (World Bank, 1988). In other words, the period of 1956 to 1986 was just the period Hong Kong needed to succeed fully in its industrialisation and economic development, measured in terms of the economic performance of some of the traditional, industrialised countries of the West.

Table 5 shows[2] that this development process coincides with the successful development of a textile and garment industry, starting from comparatively simple, mass-produced items such as basic cloth and cotton garments, to the highly sophisticated, high-fashion industry that is rightly associated with Hong Kong today.

In 1956, only a few years after the beginning of industrial manufacturing in Hong Kong, the textiles and garments accounted for 68.6 per cent of Hong Kong's total exports, out of which textiles accounted for more than two-thirds. Table 5 shows further that textile manufacturing, i.e. cloth, by 1966, had been overtaken as the most important industry by garment manufacturing. The latter reached its peak share of the manufacturing sector in 1976, and then declined to 33.9 per cent in 1986.

---

[2]Table 5 shows exports, rather than production data. But the size of the domestic market of Hong Kong has from the beginning been negligible compared to the export market for textiles and garments.

Table 5. Composition of Hong Kong's Exports, 1956 – 1986

	Value (HK$ Million %)				
Major Items	1956(1)	1966(2)	1976(3)	1984(4)	1986(5)
Clothing	21.1	40.0	44.8	34.6	33.9
Textiles	47.5	16.4	9.4	6.3	7.1
Electronic and electrical	8.2	10.5	14.8	24.3	22.5
Machinery & transport equipment	–	0.1	0.1	0.1	0.1
Plastic products (including plastic toys and games)	1.2	13.2	9.0	0.6	9.0
Watches and clocks and precision	–	1.3	5.2	7.8	8.9
Metal products	5.6	5.4	2.6	2.3	2.3
Jewellery, precious stones, wigs etc.	–	1.6	1.5	1.5	2.1
Travel bags and handbags	–	1.0	2.1	1.5	1.0
Household equipment	10.8	0.1	0.1	0.1	0.7
Other	5.6	9.6	9.4	9.8	12.4
Total	100.0	100.0	100.0	100.0	100.0

Sources: 1. *Annual Department Reports* 1956–57, Director of Commerce & Industry, Hong Kong Government, p. 47

2. *Review of Overseas Trade* 1966, Commerce and Industry Department, Hong Kong Government, p. 30–31

3. *Annual Statistical Review* 1972–76, Commerce & Industry Department, Hong Kong Government, p. 6–7.

4. *Annual Statistical Review*, 1984, Trade Department, Hong Kong Government, p. 4–5.

5. *Annual Statistical Review*, 1986, Trade Department, Hong Kong Government, p. 4–5

Regardless of this relative decline, Hong Kong's garment industry was still by far the most important manufacturing industry in 1986, employing about fifty per cent of the industrial workforce, some 450,000 workers out of a total industrial workforce of 870,000. This continued importance of the textile and garment industry is also born out by the role of this industrial branch in world trade and Hong Kong's share in it. Total world trade in textiles and garments comprises Standard Industrial Trade Classifications (SITC) 26 plus 65 plus 84. Between 1970 and 1991, the value of trade in these categories grew from US$24.8 billion to US$257.8 billion, i.e. by about ten times in twenty years. Also in 1991, Hong Kong's trade in these product categories was valued at US$28.7 billion, more than total world trade only twenty years ago.

What had changed in the 1970s, was not the importance of the textile and garment industry, but the application of the model of production for exports that had worked so well for textiles and garments, to other light industrial goods, especially electronics and electrical goods, plastic products, and watches, clocks and precision instruments. Table 5 shows the rise of these three industries as well. They all started later than the textiles and garment industry, and also peaked later.

Following the earlier suggestion that Macau's economic development is best analysed as part of Hong Kong, we now add and integrate the former into the emerging picture. For the first six decades of the twentieth century, Macau had relied on local handicraft type of industries, like the production of matches, fire-crackers, and incense. As late as 1958, their share in Macau's exports was still around forty per cent. Fishing provided about one-third of Macau's exports. All this indicates, above all, that exports from Macau were small, and certainly insufficient to generate any significant level of wealth comparable with that of Hong Kong (Sit, Cremer, and Wong, 1991).

Macau's major thrust in the development of a modern economy was the result of Hong Kong's success. There was, from the 1960s, pressure of increasing trade restrictions, first from the United Kingdom, then by the United States and the European Economic Community, on Hong Kong exports, initially cotton products. In consequence, Hong Kong entrepreneurs sought to establish production facilities in nearby Macau, which was at that time under no restrictions. During the 1960s, Macau's textile and garment industry grew at annual rates of up to fifty per cent, benefiting from Hong Kong investment, and the GSP (General System of Preferences) status, which granted preferential tariffs in the importing economies for selected products originating from developing countries. Around 1970, more countries introduced trade restrictions on Hong Kong. The range of restricted products became more and more extended. A particular factor in the development of Macau's export industry was the withdrawal of GSP status from Hong Kong.

Investing in Macau became the obvious and viable response of Hong Kong manufacturers. The majority of factories are owned and operated by Hong Kong entrepreneurs, with managers and technical supervisors brought in from there. Nam Kwong Co., as the semi-official representative of China's commercial interests in Macau, estimated that in the 20 years up to 1985, a total of two billion Macau patacas had been invested in Macau from foreign sources. Of this sum, 70 per cent is believed to have come from Hong Kong. 60 per cent of Macau's industrial investment originated from Hong Kong, according to a further source (Almanac, 1986: 26). Edmonds (1994: 27) similarly estimates that only one quarter of Macau's investment is domestic investment. This ownership and management structure appears to justify the treatment of Macau as an economic satellite of Hong Kong.

Regardless of the ownership and the control issue associated with it, Macau repeated the development pattern of Hong Kong. In the 1970s, and almost twenty years later than in Hong Kong, the textile and garment sector, which had spilled over from Hong Kong, was the driving force of export-driven economic growth in Macau. Their share in total exports grew from 58.2 per cent in 1970 to nearly 90 per cent in 1979. Total exports grew at an average annual growth rate of 27 per cent in the decade. As in Hong Kong, the textiles and garment industry was followed by a second generation of light industrial production. In Macau, these were plastic toys, electronics and electrical products, and artificial flowers. They reached a combined share of around 30 per cent, but then stagnated (Feitor and Cremer, 1991: 184). Still, Macau's industry is small compared with Hong Kong's. The value of exports of textiles and garments in 1991 was US$1.3 billion, compared to Hong Kong's US$28.7 billion.

The main destinations of goods from Hong Kong and Macau changed over the period under consideration. Tables 6 and 7 show the destination of exports from Hong Kong and Macau, respectively, for the period of 1950 to 1990 as shares of total exports. The bottom line also gives the total value itself.

Table 6 shows, first of all, that in 1950, i.e. the post-war entrepot economy, 77.9 per cent of all export trade was destined for Asian markets. Trade with Asian countries was almost ten times as important as trade with either North America or Western Europe. By far the most important trading partner was China, which alone accounted for 33.9 per cent of Hong Kong's export markets. It is worth noting that Macau, as Hong Kong's immediate neighbour, accounted for a substantial share of Hong Kong's exports — 5.6 per cent, a bigger share than any other Asian economy, with the obvious exception of China. This last information shows perhaps that the internationalisation of Hong Kong's economy had not yet reached global dimensions. This is also evident from the fact that a

Table 6. Destinations of Exports from Hong Kong, 1950 – 1990

	1950	1960	1970	1980	1990
North America (%)	8.6	21.6	38.4	28.1	26.0
Western Europe (%)	9.2	22.2	25.4a	26.3a	19.9a
Asia (%)	77.9	39.0	23.0b	34.1b	43.8
thereof:					
China (%)	33.95	3.0	..	8.2	24.8
Macau (%)	5.6	1.7	1.0	1.0	..
Others (%)	4.3	17.2	13.2	11.5	10.3
Total (HK$'000,000)	3,716	3,938	15,238	98,242	639,874

Sources: Hong Kong Statistics 1947 – 1967, Census and Statistics Department, Hong Kong 1969; 1974 and 1993 *International Trade Statistics Yearbook, Vol. 1, Trade by Country*, New York, United Nations: 1976 and 1995; and own calculations from these data.

Notes: (a) EEC plus EFTA; (b) A change in the statistical concept of what is included in "Asia" made it impossible to be totally consistent, and an adjustment, based on the 1990 data, was employed; ".." denotes a value of less than 0.5 per cent

mere 4.3 per cent of total trade was with countries other than those explicitly accounted for in Table 6. Obviously, regional trade, especially with close, well-known neighbours, still dominated the foreign economic relations.

By 1960, the transition from entrepot to global trading economy was clearly visible. The total export volume was only slightly higher than a decade ago, indicating the difficulty of the transition. The trade with China had virtually collapsed to a mere 3.0 per cent, and was less than one-tenth of the 1950 value. Similarly, and probably also for political reasons, the trade with Macau had shrunk to one-third of its former value. The loss of the Chinese and the Macau market almost entirely explains the drop of export markets in Asia, which had otherwise remained quite stable. The significant change was the increased importance of both the North American and European markets, to 21.6 and 22.2 per cent, respectively, and a noticeable reaching out to other economies in the world.

This trend continued over a considerable period. Total trade value increased about fourfold from 1960 to 1970. In 1970, exports to North America reached 38.4 per cent of all export trade, and the trade to Europe also increased further to 25.4 per cent. Simultaneously, exports to China had become negligible, and the cross border trade with Macau, although higher than before in absolute terms, no longer played a significant role for Hong Kong. The importance of North America especially had grown so fast that the share of exports to Asia had fallen to 23.0 per cent.

The data for 1980 reflect a number of important developments. Trade expansion was even faster than in the 1960s: The overall trade value increased about sixfold. But the newly expanding markets were now in Asia, especially in China. Exports to the "traditional" market in North America increased at a slower pace, mainly because of trade restrictions. This emergence of Asia as the most important market for Hong Kong exports continued throughout the 1980s. Exports to the United States stabilised at around a quarter of Hong Kong's total exports. European markets fell in importance, while Asian markets further gained. By 1990, with another sixfold increase of total trade within ten years, China alone accounted for 24.8 per cent[3] of Hong Kong's exports, a very significant part of which is again, as had traditionally been the case, re-export trade.

Table 7 contains information which complements the analysis of Hong Kong's export trade from 1950 to 1990 with data for Macau.

Table 7 reveals the development lag of Macau, compared with Hong Kong, which we have already discussed. The data for 1960 show the historically inherited, colonial trade pattern: 44.0 per cent of Macau's exports were to Portugal, and 37.0 per cent to neighbouring Hong Kong. Total trade was insignificant at 56 million Macau patacas.[4] By 1970 the beginnings of Macau's industrialisation process along the model already successfully implemented in Hong Kong were evident. Portugal's share had plummeted by more than half, and export trade with developed market economies had begun. The European Community absorbed 34.5 per cent of Macau's still very low total export value of 256 million patacas, equivalent to about US$42 million.

---

[3]China's share further increased to 32.3 per cent in 1993.

[4]It is not likely that there should have been no trade with China in this period. However, it is possible that due to the unclear international status of Macau, trade data were not made public. In any case, most of Macau's trade with China at the time would have been cross-border trade with the Guangdong Province.

Table 7. Destinations of Exports from Macau, 1960 – 1990

	1960	1970	1980	1990
U.S.A. (%)	7.5	8.7	19.6	36.0a
European Community (%)	1.0b	34.5b	54.2b	34.2
Portugal (%)	44.0	29.3	3.1	..
Asia (%)	n.a.	n.a.	n.a.	n.a.
thereof:				
China (%)	..	..	0.2	4.5
Hong Kong (%)	37.0	17.9	12.5	13.1
Others				
Total ('000,000 patacas)	56	256	2,742	21,131

Sources: Director of Statistics and Census: Almanac of Macau's Economy, 1986; 1993 *International Trade Statistics Yearbook, Vol. 1, Trade by Country,* New York, United Nations: 1995, and own calculations from these data.

Notes: (a) includes Canada; (b) does not include Portugal; ".." denotes a value of less than 0.5 per cent; n.a. denotes that the data are not available.

The development pattern of Macau from 1970 onwards followed that of Hong Kong. A difference was that Macau developed the European market for its exports faster than its North American market. Cultural, legal and language differences may have influenced this. In 1980, more than half (54.2 per cent) of Macau's exports were shipped to Europe, whereas Europe never had more than a quarter of Hong Kong's exports. It appears, however, that Macau developed the United States market later as well. In 1990, the latter had overtaken Europe. On the Asian markets, Macau is much less active and successful than Hong Kong. This may be due to the fact that the lag has meant that other Asian economies are competitors of Macau, rather than markets for its products, especially in the textiles and garments trade.

The relevance of the industrialisation pattern emerging from these observations is not to be underestimated. The textile and garment industries are ideally suited to early industrialisation. They require a large work force, relatively little technology and capital, and they are important international commodities, where cost advantages are decisive. In combination with export-orientation, the production of textiles and garments enables developing countries to industrialise on a significant scale, and to diversify into other products and markets.

Hong Kong, with Macau in its wake, has been the most successful case of this development concept. A growing number of developing countries, not only but especially in East and Southeast Asia, have imitated a development path similar to that of Hong Kong.

The relocation of production facilities from both Hong Kong and Macau into Southern China from the mid-1980s onwards is a good example. But at almost the same time, Malaysia and Thailand, and more recently, Vietnam and Laos, are copying the model.

2.2.3 *The policy framework*

Factors underlying the success of export-oriented industrialisation, with special reference to the newly industrialising economies of Southeast Asia, have been discussed extensively in the literature. Chen's *Hyper-Growth in Asian Economies* (1979) is one of the original works. James, Naya, and Meier (1987) provide a comprehensive overview in *Asian Development: Economic Success and Policy Lessons*. Landsberg (1987) takes a more critical perspective in his essay *Export-led Industrialisation in the Third World: Manufacturing Imperialism*. And a comprehensive report on the Asian growth experience based on this model is provided in the World Bank Policy Research Report, *The East Asian Miracle* (1993a).

It appears that most of the literature emphasises policies and institutional factors as the main determinants. For example, the World Bank identifies two broad lessons of success in the high-performing Asian economies. These two factors are: Adherence to market-oriented principles, and carefully selected policy interventions.

> "Their {the HPAE's) rapid growth had two complementary elements. First, getting the fundamentals right was essential. Without high levels of domestic savings, broadly based human capital, good macro economic management, and limited price distortions, there would have been no basis for growth and no means by which the gains of rapid productivity change could have been realised. Policies to assist the financial sector capture non financial savings and to

> increase household and corporate savings were central. Acquisition of technology through openness to direct foreign investment and licensing were crucial to rapid productivity growth. Public investment complemented private investment and increased its orientation to exports. Education policies stressed universal primary schooling and improvements in quality at primary and secondary levels.
>
> Second, very rapid growth of the type experienced by Japan, the Four Tigers, and more recently the East Asian NIEs has at times benefited from careful policy interventions. All interventions carry costs, either in the direct fiscal costs of subsidies or foregone revenues, or the implicit taxation of households and firms, for example, through tariffs or interest rate controls. Unlike many other governments that attempted such interventions, HPAE governments generally held costs within well-defined limits. ... Given the overriding importance ascribed to macroeconomic stability, interventions that became too costly or otherwise threatened stability were quickly modified and abandoned." (World Bank, 1993a: op.cit. 24–25)

James, Naya, and Meier (1987: 18–22) list five factors:

- Market or private sector-oriented approach to support outward-looking development strategies
- Elimination of price distortions in the national economies — to correspond to conditions on the international markets
- Cautious fiscal and financial management
- Priority to economic growth over social welfare spending
- Flexibility

Feitor and Cremer (1991: 189) also list five favourable factors and conditions that have been significant for the development of Macau's economy, although only the first two of the factors they list are policy-related:

- Liberal economic system, with limited government intervention and very low tax burden
- Comparatively favourable access to foreign markets

- Favourable geographical location, especially the proximity to Hong Kong, which makes possible the spill-over effects of Hong Kong's development, and to mainland China, which provides cheap sources of food, other necessities and raw materials
- High elasticity of labour supply, which allows wage levels to be kept comparatively low, coupled with the relatively high quality of labour for jobs not very demanding in skills
- Existence of a nucleus of dynamic entrepreneurs with a positive attitude towards risk-assumption and a reasonable knowledge of the export markets

While some economists (e.g. Cline, 1982) have pointed out that initial conditions are crucial, and that the model cannot therefore be easily copied, this is not the prevailing view. Most analyses suggest that:

> "inappropriate macroeconomic and trade policies have been the bane of economic development in many developed countries, while export-oriented growth and suitable macroeconomic policies have been mutually supportive aspects of economic success" (James, Naya, and Meier 1987: 234).

This emphasis on policies, i.e. the insistence that the organisation of an economic system is man-made, is tempting, because it suggests that the successful model can be copied by applying those policies. It would appear though, that the negative proposition that inappropriate policies and institutional arrangements are most harmful to development, is much stronger than the inverse positive formulation. This suggests that macroeconomic policies and institutional arrangements are necessary, but not sufficient, for economic development. In terms of the theory of industrial organisation, and with specific reference to the earlier discussion about the interlinkages between high-level and lower-level organisation, this suggests that we must look at the other organisational levels next.

2.3 Industrial Structure and Business Characteristics

Many authors, economists and sociologists make reference to the importance of factors below the macro-level. As shown above, Feitor and Cremer (1991) include micro-level factors, in that they emphasise the need for a certain form of risk-taking entrepreneurship, as well as the need for detailed, i.e. product and market specific, knowledge. Wong (1986) analysed the role of entrepreneurs, coming from a sociocultural perspective.

The industrial structure of Hong Kong and Macau was the subject of a seven-year international research project on *The Changes in the Industrial Structure and the Role of Small and Medium Industries in Asian Countries*, funded by the Institute of Developing Economies, Tokyo (1984–1990). This large project also included research projects in Hong Kong, Macau, and the Guangdong Province of China (Sit and Wong 1989; Sit, Cremer and Wong, 1991; Cremer, 1991a; Sit and Wong, 1990).

In at least three ways, that project, or rather, that interrelated series of projects, was a precursor of the project which is the subject of this monograph. Firstly, it studied empirically the industrial structure of export-oriented economies on the level of industry (textiles, garments, electronics, etc.), and the level of business organisations (small and medium scale firms). In terms of our current perspective on the industrial organisation of trading economies, this project was therefore aimed at the second tier of the overall organisation of trading economies, focusing mainly on manufacturing enterprises. Secondly, the interest in the current project grew partly out of the earlier one, in that the latter did not address the activity of trading. This seemed to leave both a clear gap in the knowledge and understanding of how a trading economy works, and it also did not study trade at the lowest, "most fundamental" (Milgrom and Roberts 1992: 21) level of the transactions themselves. Thirdly, the personal knowledge of, and familiarity with, companies in both Hong Kong and Macau was a valuable starting point for the selection of companies included in the present project.

This 1984–1990 project provided valuable insights into

- the changes in industrial structure that accompany successful industrialisation
- the problems faced by small and medium scale enterprises
- the potential of small and medium enterprises in terms of income creation, employment generation, and technology transfer
- policies directly aimed at supporting enterprises

A brief synopsis of the results of the earlier project may be sufficient here. The study focused on entrepreneurs, the enterprises they built, the industrial organisation of the manufacturing sector, and the role they play in the process of export-oriented economic development. The project included all nine economies: South Korea, Singapore, Malaysia, the Philippines, Indonesia, Pakistan, Hong Kong, Macau, and the Guangdong Province of the People's Republic of China. Topics dealt with included a sociological and ethnographic profile of the Chinese entrepreneurs, their training and education and their management style and self-perception. Furthermore, age, development history, size, location, and ownership characteristics of manufacturing establishments were studied in detail. Issues of funding, labour and labour relations, technology employed, products and markets, were also discussed. Finally, non-market inter-firm relationships within the domestic economy, and internationally, typically via subcontracting relationships, were investigated as well.

Out of the study emerged an interesting and perhaps suggestive image of small economies, reacting flexibly, sometimes in a rather reactive fashion, to cope with volatilities, uncertainties, and dependencies largely beyond their control. There appears to have developed an industrial system with a set of flexible and adaptive coping mechanisms. This system appeared to have been essential to the successful development of Hong Kong and Macau. Perhaps the two main characteristics of the industrial structure of Hong Kong and Macau are the inevitability of dependencies, and the limited knowledge and skill base of the manufacturing enterprises.

The dependencies and uncertainties that pervade the export-industries of Hong Kong and Macau are multiple and interconnected, and they conform to the general linkages between different levels of the industrial organisations, which we outlined above. They begin with the general dependence of these economies upon the international markets, and then a dependence on each other. Firms are dependent upon on international trade agreements, on government regulations, and on overseas trading companies. Smaller firms are dependent on larger firms, through formal or informal subcontracting relationships, and upon each other. Individual entrepreneurs are dependent upon personal business relationships, goodwill, perceived mutual benefit, and upon their families and friends.

The project also left no doubt about a lack of the kind of training and expertise that one would normally consider essential to run businesses successfully. This is evident in, among other things, blatant ignorance about management principles, production technology, about financial matters, and, amazingly, the international markets they want to serve. Sit, Cremer, and Wong (1991: 204) summarise:

> "Generally, the entrepreneurs are poorly trained in terms of both general education and specific technical and managerial competencies and they do not lay much store by that. Neither do they, as a generality, possess much relevant experience in operating a manufacturing business. They also generally have family backgrounds that for the most part could be described as irrelevant to their being entrepreneurs. It also could be said that they have rather limited conceptions of the skills required to run a business."

Both of these characteristics, dependency and lack of knowledge and skill, have led many authors to doubt the ability of these economies to attain lasting, sustainable success — a hypothesis manifestly at odds with the facts.

Hayek warned of the fallacy of "overpure economists" (1936: 44), trying to explain why something might not work in the face of a remarkably successful reality, and pointed to the role of pure equilibrium analysis in causing this fallacy. Referring to the heroic assumptions about the acquisition and communication of relevant knowledge that have to be made in order to explain how market equilibrium can ever be achieved, he warned:

> "The situation seems to be that, before we can explain why people commit mistakes, we must first explain why they should ever be right." (Hayek 1936: 34)

We submit that the apparent paradox results from a failure to recognise the interaction of various layers, and hence the division of labour, within the industrial organisation of trading economies. In particular there is a failure to look in sufficient depth into the trading end of the process. Instead, the focus is on production, technology transfer as far as enterprises are concerned, and on institutional arrangements, as far as markets are concerned. This is, of course, in the best tradition of classical economics: In a perfectly competitive market, transaction costs are assumed to be equal to zero, with voluntary exchange leading to maximum social utility. Prices are assumed to provide adequate and sufficient signals for buyers and sellers to agree on transactions. Trading, i.e. the activities required to come to an agreement between seller and buyer, is not an issue in this economic model.

In reality, the process of mediation, and the skills and competencies required to perform the mediation successfully and dependably, may hold the key to the success or failure of international trading, and the economic development that comes with it.

2.4 Trade Transactions and Trading Companies

The very high level of abstraction of economic analysis, that is carried out under the label of the "theory of the firm", is one in which:

> "firms act like single decision-makers guided by prices and costs, buying labour and other inputs in impersonal spot markets, converting them into output via given and largely unchanging technologies, and selling this production in more impersonal markets." (Milgrom and Roberts 1992: 594)

This level of abstraction, while certainly useful for a number purposes, simply does not do for the reality of international trade transactions in textiles and garments, and probably not in too many others either. For example (Milgrom and Roberts, 1992: 31),

> "if the product is wheat, then the contract may simply specify that a fixed amount of a standardised grade of grain (for example, Manitoba 1 Northern hard wheat) will be delivered at a particular date (say, 1 April, 1992) and place (say, Winnipeg) for a specified price (for example, $5 Canadian per bushel). The basic contract is then very simple. In contrast, a contract to build a power plant for an electric utility is very complicated. The utility's estimate of demand may change during construction, and the cost and availability of fuel may change as well. The environmental impact of the facility may be unknown at the outset, and the cost of providing the necessary environmental and health and safety safeguards may be unpredictable. The right way to proceed, the length of time to take, and whether to finish the project at all are decisions to be made later, after the contract is signed and execution begins."

In the latter case, independence of producer/seller and buyer/consumer is an abstraction. Obviously, in the case of the power plant, the production of the product itself is dependent on continuous communication and coordination of seller and buyer. If this coordination and communication does not take place, the product cannot be created to any required standards, and not to the satisfaction of either side.

International trade transactions are of this nature as well. Transactions in textiles and garments are a combination of routine and uniqueness. On the one hand, they are so standardised and routine that they could be said to constitute a script, in the sense made familiar by Thorndyke (1977), which is repeated in every trade transaction all over again. On the other hand, because of the unique nature of each individual textile product, as well as the uniqueness of the countries, companies and people involved in any given trade transaction, this basic and rigid script is played out differently every time. There are problems of product specification, shipment and packing details, time schedules, financing and guarantees, which require solutions strictly on a case-by-case basis.

Chapters 3, 4 and 5 of this book will show in detail and analyse how trade transactions, while following a fundamentally unchanging pattern, are realised and created as unique and distinct business deals every time a trade transaction takes place in reality. The concept of the trade transaction as an exchange between buyer and seller, who both possess perfect knowledge about the product in question and focus their concerns on prices, exists only on a very high level of abstraction, certainly in relation to textiles and garment products.

2.4.1 *The structure of trade transactions*

The structure of trade transactions as related to textiles and garments in Hong Kong and Macau is set out below, and taken, with minor modifications only, from Cremer and Willes (1991: 104-108).

Trade transactions consist of several sequential stages, some of which are optional, while most of them are obligatory. The purpose of describing the various stages of trade transactions in detail is that they relate directly and obviously to the need for communication between the two parties to the transaction, so that they may acquire the information needed to progress the respective deal to the next stage and eventually to completion. The central role of communication in achieving the desired economic outcome will thus become obvious.

The first stage of a trade transaction may be called *Ordering*. The objective of this first stage is to establish an agreement between the buyer and the manufacturer to produce and absorb a textile product of well-defined quality and quantity, within a certain time frame. The ordering may start from both ends. Either the potential buyer, touring Southeast Asia in search for a producer, provides a sample and any further instructions, or the producer advertises a sample with some comments as to what he could produce. Typically, the buyer and the producer do not communicate directly with each other: they do not, as a rule, know each other, and even if they do, they do not normally have any common language. Instead, both producer and buyer use the services of traders. Traders include independent trading companies, buying offices which normally act on behalf of one major buyer only, or trading departments of major producers. The original offer will normally be submitted to the trader in the native language of the requester, on the assumption, grounded in experience, that it will be understood by the trader, if necessary, with the help of a translator. The trading company will then contact, sometimes following specific requests, a manufacturer or buyer, as the case may be. Negotiation follows, and a provisional order, with size-sets, quantities, packaging requirements and time schedules, where these are appropriate, may follow. There may be fabric swatches or photographs to be sent before a formal contract is drawn up. Although the buyer may have visited the manufacturer on some occasion, the negotiation is made through and with the help of middlemen, and involves communication in at least two, often three, different languages, for example, German, Chinese (Cantonese), and as a bridge, English, where understanding falters. It is worth noting from the start that written documents accompany, and are indeed indispensable to, every stage of the process.

A confirmed order is the final step in the first stage, either in English, or in the buyer's language, or both. Once the contract is signed, the first stage of ordering is regarded by both parties as completed by a binding agreement, and the product is "free for production". In principle, it would appear that the next interaction between manufacturer and buyer could be the delivery of the goods, as agreed, followed by payment settlement, along the lines of the wheat example, above, cf. page 47. In reality, the most important interaction between manufacturer and buyer has just begun.

Once the order is confirmed, there are largely two parallel sequences of action to be executed, each of them accompanied and overseen by a third sequence, the full documentation of the monitoring and control process. The first one is the physical production and delivery of the product. The second one is trade finance. Both sequences are essential parts of the entire trade transaction, and their precise realisation and implementation, as the transaction unfolds, fulfills the contract agreed upon. Consequently, from this stage onwards, documentation and clear understanding are crucial. All important communication between manufacturer and buyer, via the trader, is in English. We shall see the importance of written documentation in English most clearly when we turn to trade finance, but it is also evident from the process of production and delivery, which we look at next.

Manufacture is the stage that follows *Ordering*. It is for the supplier to prepare a manufacturing order. This may run to several pages. It must include, of course, details of size-sets, number of items, design, fabric, etc., and it may include detailed diagrams and working drawings. The form on which it is prepared has headings in English, making it internationally identifiable for all participants. But the form is only for use in one locality: the manufacturer's. Therefore, the text is entirely in Chinese, since it has to be used by a workforce which cannot be expected to be able to read any other language besides the local one. During this time, the merchandiser of the trading company acts as a broker between the producer and the buyer using English — an English both heavily contextualised and specialised, which will be elaborated upon below.

Once the product is near completion, a new stage sets in, that of *Inspection*. The manufacturer will inform the merchandiser, who acts on the buyer's behalf and in his best interests, that the goods are ready for inspection, regardless of any quality control that the manufacturer may have in place inside his own factory. Inspection is done by random sampling, and is normally recorded by means of a Quality Control form provided by the buyer. The form is in English and, possibly, another European language, for example French. It is designed to ensure rapid and thorough recording of every detail of manufacture, the purpose being to use it as a basis for amendments, alterations, or rejections. In many cases, it is only at this stage that the quality and potential markets can be properly assessed and prices can be decided upon: what may have looked good on the order form and suitable for sale in boutiques in Europe may turn out to be better suited to be produced in larger quantities and fewer colours for department stores. At first sight it may seem that the completion of the Quality Control forms by someone whose control of either of its languages is at best no more than partial, would be almost impossibly difficult — yet it is routinely achieved with the help of the merchandisers. Difficulties do however arise, and the study of these, and of the means by which they are resolved, is instructive to the processes of communication involved.

The next action in the sequence of production and delivery is that of *Shipment*. The shipment details are part of the agreement between buyer and manufacturer, and are spelled out precisely in the contract. The contract may, for example, include not only the shipping company to be used and the dates, but also in much detail the packaging and the agencies to be employed. The process requires the completion of a number of documents, including the Bill of Lading, the Certificate of Origin, the Export License, the Shipment Certificate, etc.

While all this has been unfolding, a different but related sequence has been developing, that of *Trade Finance*. Only in rare cases will a manufacturer pre-finance the materials needed and produce according to order, and almost never will he wait for payment until after the goods, which are consumer items in the case of textiles and garments, are sold to the end-users by the buyer. There are two reasons for this: Firstly, the manufacturer may not have the financial resources to finance production in advance, and secondly, he may not be sure of the buyer's ability to pay, i.e. his chances of selling the goods on the (foreign) market. This is why trade finance, by the way of using documentary credits, is needed and is in common use.

Trade finance by way of Letters of Credit is a particularly interesting part of the entire trade transaction, because it rests on documents only. The Letter of Credit is opened by the buyer, through two or more banks, in favour of the manufacturer, normally once the order is confirmed. It is essentially a promise to pay the manufacturer on presentation of trade documents — not on delivery of the goods — as agreed in the credit contract. The bank, therefore, gives a loan to the buyer, once the supplier has provided documentary evidence that he has fulfilled his part of the contract. A similar credit procedure can be used by the manufacturer to finance the purchase of raw materials, say, fabrics from Taiwan.

A Letter of Credit is highly formalised, and specifies, always in English, exactly and in much detail, the obligations of the manufacturer regarding product, time schedules, shipment, etc. The entire trade transaction, at least all its essential details are, because of the nature of the credit, precisely documented. This is necessary, because the bank arranges payment on presentation only of documents, regardless of any business reality. The significance of the Letter of Credit is that if the conditions set out in it are not fulfilled to the letter, the bank, and hence the buyer, may refuse, on documentary evidence alone, to pay the manufacturer. As the bank is not required to check[5] more than superficially the correctness of the respective documents, a full understanding of its contents on the part of the manufacturer is required for his need and his claim to be paid for the work done.

If the buyer is satisfied in all respects with the goods received, the payment made by the banks as the final part of the trade transaction will stand.

However, if the buyer is not satisfied with the goods received, a claim, supported by inspection documents, may follow. Claims are not uncommon. A compromise acceptable to both parties is normally reached by the offer of a discount in consideration of either bad workmanship or one or more missing items. In some cases, for example when items have gone missing, this may be a matter for the buyer's insurer, not for the manufacturer.

2.4.2 *Merchandisers and communication*

With the individual trade transaction as the unit of analysis, it becomes possible to trace the unfolding of every phase of it. One important observation stands out, which corresponds to the industrial organisation literature. This observation is the central role of communication in trade transaction, and the importance of individuals in it, which contrasts with the pure economic theory of exchanges through impersonal markets, in which the need to observe and explain the communicative interaction of individuals involved in the trade transaction is

---

[5]'Banks must examine all documents with reasonable care to ascertain that they appear on their face to be in accordance with the terms and conditions of the credit. Documents which appear on their face to be inconsistent with one another will be considered as not appearing on their face to be in accordance with the terms and conditions of the credit.' *Uniform Customs and Practice for Documentary Credits, published by Deutsche Bank, Frankfurt 1983, Article 13.*

replaced by an assumption of perfect, *a priori* knowledge of markets, prices, and products.

Theoretically, there are only two necessary participants in trade transactions: the seller and the buyer. Normally, the seller and the buyer are thought of as companies, whose representatives may change from time to time, but who are as individuals totally exchangeable and insubstantial to the trade transaction. The reality, which we have tried to describe in the previous section, is quite different.

For any given transaction in the international textile and garment trade to come about, a continuous flow of communication between seller and buyer is required at every single stage of the transaction. Each deal is accompanied by communication, mostly written communication in the form of facsimile messages, used to control and monitor the deal from its earliest stage to its completion.

The constant and interesting fact of international trade business in and with Asia is that the seller and buyer do not speak nor write each other's language, and have generally very little understanding of each other's culture and code of behaviour. In the case of Hong Kong and Macau, the sellers are speakers of Cantonese, as are their employees who do the actual work of manufacture according to the required specifications. Their understanding of European or North American markets and business practices is very limited, as the studies of Sit and Wong (1989) and Sit, Cremer, and Wong (1991) show for both economies under consideration. The buyers are speakers of European languages, usually (American) English or French or German. Their understanding of Asian business practices and of the conditions of manufacturing in Hong Kong and Macau is also limited. The booming market for internationally popular books on 'how-to-do-business-in-Asia', sympathetically and well reviewed by Julian (1990), is indicative of the degree of ignorance. The situation is further complicated in the case of Macau, where the language of government, and therefore of government business, including the control of export business, is Portuguese.

Continued, reliable, and quick communication under these conditions appears almost impossibly difficult — yet it works nearly all the time because of the ever-present middleman.

This third, theoretically dispensable, but practically indispensable middleman is a trading company, which is usually a small firm with less than ten, often less than five employees. There are many varieties of trading companies, ranging from relatively large buying offices, to small export departments belonging to large manufacturing companies. Quite often, large trading companies own factories themselves. The basic function of the middleman, however, remains unchanged, and in practice, is assumed by a person employed by the trading company and known as a *merchandiser*. The basic role is to mediate between seller and buyer. This *process of mediation* between the producer/seller and the customer/buyer is the essence of trading. It, and hence international trade, is dependent on and linked to language and communication systems.

The spread of fax machines, cheap and reliable telephone links, and computer data links have revolutionised the exchange of information, and complement the improvements in transportation technology, as well as the reductions of barriers to trade and investment. The study of international trade transactions must take this changed environment into account.

2.5 The Analysis of International Trade Transactions

The process of mediation, i.e. the continuous flow of communication between seller and buyer at every single stage of every single trade transaction, incurs costs. Transaction cost economics understands organisations to be devices which minimise transaction costs. Firms are in many cases the best organisational mode to economise on transaction costs, as opposed to all individuals working independently and for themselves.

While the idea is appealing, the nature of transaction costs is actually not very well understood. The reason for this is that in many cases the nature of the transactions themselves, which go on in and between organisations, are not well understood. More specifically, we do not know well enough and not in sufficient detail, what, for example, the completion of an international trade deal in 20,000 ladies' silk blouses, entails. And therefore, we do not know what actually accounts for the costs of the respective transaction. Put differently, the production functions of many transactions are not known.

> "[Attention] is focused on economising efforts that attend the organisation of transactions — where a transaction occurs when a good or service is transferred across a technologically separable

> interface. One stage of activity terminates and another begins. With a well-working interface, as with a well-working machine, these transfers occur smoothly. In mechanical systems we look for frictions: do the gears mesh, are the parts lubricated, is there needless slippage or other loss of energy? The economic counterpart of friction is transaction cost: for that subset of transactions where it is important to elicit cooperation,* do the parties to the exchange operate harmoniously, or are there frequent misunderstandings and conflicts that lead to delays, breakdowns and other malfunctions? Transaction cost analysis entails an examination of the comparative costs of planning, adapting, and monitoring task completion under alternative governance structures." (Williamson 1989: 142)

The footnote (*) in the quoted passage of text is also important. Williamson (ibidem) adds in this footnote that the

> "genius of neoclassical economics is that there are large numbers of transactions where conscious cooperation is not necessary. The invisible hand works well if each party can go its own way — the buyer can secure product easily from alternative sources; the supplier can redeploy his assets without loss of productive value — with little cost to the other. Transaction cost economics is concerned with the frictions that obtain when bilateral dependency intrudes. This is not a trivial class of activity."

Bilateral dependency of buyer and seller, evidenced through continuous interaction and communication between them, is the essence of international trade in textiles and garments.[6]

The transactions which are the subject of our study are encoded in written English, that has been retained for reasons not related to our research requirements, but the purposes of the participants. These retained texts enable

---

[f]Hayek goes much further than this. He suggests in *Economics and Knowledge* that the concept of market equilibrium is applied only without major difficulty to the actions of one single person. As soon as two or more individuals are involved in a transaction, compatibility of plans and expectations as to the nature of the exchange, e.g. the properties of the product, cannot be assumed but must be communicated between them (Hayek, 1949: 35–39)

us to study the unfolding of each of the above phases of a trade transaction. This will show that every phase of an international trade transaction is accompanied by communication, normally written text, used to coordinate the transaction from beginning to completion. In terms of the units of organisational theory, we do not stop with the transaction as the lowest and most fundamental unit of analysis, but we look at an even smaller unit of analysis: we look at the fine detail of the communication which defines and in a sense creates the deal between seller and buyer of a product by a mechanism different and distinct from the price mechanism. We argue that communication, in addition to prices, is a principal and indispensable coordination mechanism in the creation of trade business, that international trade, to quote again the catch phrase from Cope and Solomon (1993), 'runs on talk.'

With this approach we position our research within the framework of the institutional structure of production, as defined by Coase (1992), and as a contribution to the research programme he outlined in his Nobel Prize lecture in 1991 (Coase, 1992: 719, emphasis added):

> "I have come to the conclusion that the main obstacle faced by researchers of industrial organisation is the lack of data on *contracts and the activities of firms*."

Chapters 3 to 5 present and discuss in much detail the empirical data of trade transactions, encoded in written communication, which we have collected from Hong Kong and Macau trading companies.

Chapter 3

The Language of International Trade Deals

In this chapter, the focus narrows to the consideration of data relating to particular trade transactions encoded in written English. We are concerned with the fine detail of company transactions, with the activity and interaction of individuals, and specifically with what we earlier identified as the continuous communication and co-ordination between buyer and supplier by which deals are initiated, negotiated, and brought to completion. Together, these details constitute the micro-fabric of international trade.

The unit of investigation is the *transaction* — a term used commonly in economics, and one which emphasises the process of exchange which is of course central to the discipline. We prefer the term *deal* (Cremer and Willes, 1994) which is less technical, and more inclusive of all the wide variety of actions and processes that constitute international trade transactions in reality.

The chapter begins in Sec. 3.1 with a discussion of the research methodology with which we approached this study. The approach needs more than a passing reference because it is unconventional in terms of the discipline of economics (which is normally not concerned with the verbal exchanges surrounding a transaction), and the discipline of linguistics (which is normally not concerned with the logic of business and economics).

Section 3.2 classifies the data collected, not all of which are relevant to the concerns of this book. That which is centrally relevant, faxed correspondence, is the subject of Sec. 3.3. This section also includes selected illustrations from the database although a full analysis is deferred until Chapter 5. Chapter 3 concludes with a consideration of the crucial role of the middleman, the merchandiser, the intermediary and facilitator of deals, and attempts to articulate the sort of knowledge and skill that the role requires, and by which middlemen operate (Sec. 3.4).

3.1 Researching Trade Deals

3.1.1 *Trade documents*

Two conditions made practicable the access to documents that we saw as necessary to an empirical text-based investigation of the details of trade transactions. First, because communication and co-ordination are verbal processes, we are concerned with text, specifically with text transmitted via facsimile messages. Faxed text made the research feasible. Faxed exchange shares some features of verbal interaction, rapidity in particular, that the monitoring and control of manufacture and export requires. Unlike conversational interaction, however, faxed transmission leaves a retrievable trace of trade communication in the form of documents, which the companies file and preserve for their own reference, at least as long as there is any possibility of a claim in respect of the respective deal. These documents make it possible for researchers to intercept and analyse the communication related to trade deals, in particular with international trade deals, where fax is used almost to the exclusion of other modes of transmission.

Second, for well-understood historical reasons, English is the dominant language of international trade, and is the second language of the Cantonese-speaking merchandisers in Hong Kong and Macau, as it is of their suppliers and buyers based in Taiwan and elsewhere in Southeast Asia, and their other buyers, some of them international companies, some North America or Britain-based, some in Continental Europe and Scandinavia.

The earlier investigations (Sit, Cremer and Wong, 1991; Sit and Wong, 1989) of small and medium-sized enterprises in Macau and Hong Kong not only identified the topic of the research but were also instrumental in securing access to the materials. The export industry is a highly competitive business, and companies are properly protective of their own interests. Without the contacts already established, it would not have been possible for us to have virtually unconditional use of company documentation.

We are of course obliged to avoid any reference that might damage the companies' interests, and have adopted disguises for the sources of information, intended to render them unidentifiable, and briefly described at Sec. 3.1.4.

3.1.2 *An initial false start: A focus on actual expertise*

Few empirical studies proceed smoothly from inception to final report, and this one did not. An initial misconception, soon corrected by experience, was responsible for a direction we subsequently took.

We were aware, as no Europeans working in Southeast Asia can fail to be, that the English in use deviates from the Standard frequently and at every level. Initial scanning of company documents confirmed that mistakes were frequent, were neither noticed nor corrected, and were not regarded as important, nor as in any way discreditable to those responsible for them. Our initial inference was that readers of these texts were mistaken in supposing that the sense was clear and unambiguous. Writers' errors (other than minor breaches of the conventions of English orthography) necessarily obscure the sense. Confusion and ambiguity, we supposed, might go unnoticed, because readers made their own sense of the text, but the cumulative result *must* affect business negatively. Identification and elimination of at least some of the errors would benefit the companies.

This view is shared by most of those professionally engaged in teaching English for Business Purposes, and is in fact the basis of *their* business.

Consequently, our first request, once the willingness of selected companies to collaborate was established, was that they would provide access to records of *failures* of understanding, and this they agreed to do.

The unexpected result was that there was considerable difficulty for them in finding records of unmistakable failure. Success, in the sense of a satisfactory business outcome was the norm. Where failures of comprehension were located and drawn to our attention, careful scrutiny showed that they were as a rule the effect of mistaken assumptions on one side about the knowledge or experience actually in the possession of the other. They were, in short, the sort of misunderstandings that also occur between speakers in possession of effortless control of the same language. How was it, in that case, that these users who can make no ambitious claims to the mastery of English, and were entirely willing to acknowledge their limitations and to admit to frequent errors, were almost always able to arrive at a sufficient understanding for their own purposes? Were they in fact in possession of covert skills and strategies that were constantly in operation and could in principle be articulated? These seemed to us questions we should pursue in relation to our prime concern with the role and function of communication in the business of international trade.

3.1.3 *The database*

The Company Sample

No claim is made to random sampling for purposes of this study. Our choice of companies, six in Macau, four in Hong Kong, was opportunistic, and could not (given the circumstances described above) have been otherwise. The method resulted in the collection of a cumulative sample of documents of recently completed and ongoing trade deals. Subsequent study produced no evidence that they constituted two sub-samples. The belief, argued in detail in Sec. 2.2.2 above, that despite the dissimilar history of their trading operations, there are now virtually no features to distinguish Macau and Hong Kong-based companies in the textile and garment industry, was fully borne out by this experience.

Record Collection and Organisation of the Database

The collection of data had two phases, one in 1991 and a second one in 1993–4. Both were designed to assemble texts, which in the aggregate we refer to as our *database.*

We were able to introduce a Research Assistant into the companies for a period of several days in each. Bilingual in English and her native Cantonese (and of course fully bi-literate) she had, before undertaking undergraduate and graduate studies in English and Applied Linguistics, completed a diploma course in textile manufacture, and was already familiar in general terms with company routine and practice. She was asked to spend time in each company very much as a newly appointed merchandiser would do, observing the practice specific to each, making her bilingualism useful where possible, collecting documents, and noting, where possible, the remembered context of their production. She was asked to emphasise that we did not need access to sensitive material, and that we expected that the documentation we were offered would be incomplete.

After discussion of the day's work in the companies, the materials were then sorted and arranged for ease of retrieval and the pages numbered so as to preserve the order in which we received them from the companies. This order was chronological with one exception — a company that preferred to separate out incoming from outgoing faxes, and so, by disturbing the narrative, drew our attention to the *script* referred to (in Sec. 2.4, and to the *structure of a deal* described in Sec. 2.4.1).

Indexing and summary of contents was a necessary next step. Extensive paraphrase, initially a slow procedure, gave us a detailed understanding of the progress of deals towards completion, and made possible a description of the emerging variety of English that we describe in Sec. 3.2 below, and refer to as *Tradespeak*.

The first collection of 1991 comprised our initial database on trade deals, of nine companies. The tenth offered a small number of items on the first occasion, and dissociated itself from the project on the second.

We were able in 1993–1994 to return for a second series of visits. There had been changes. Of the original sample of nine, one company had virtually ceased trading in Hong Kong. Two had prospered to such an extent that our return visits were made to premises extended to accommodate an increased volume of business, and to reflect a more up-market image. Four of the nine, on this second occasion, were more closely identified with our purposes than before, and were pleased at what they perceived as a recognition of the significance of their everyday business. They provided a second set of materials more substantial and complete than what we had obtained on the first occasion, or indeed expected on the second. This material constitutes our *extended database*.

The two record collections constitute a substantial database of company records of trade deals. They make possible the reconstruction of actual trade deals, which is the subject of case studies in Chapter 4, and the studies of texts, which constitute Chapter 5.

A Note on the Anonymity of Sources

There is no compelling need for and no obvious use of the actual names under which companies trade, although the companies' names often carry some interesting meaning. Usual (but not universal) practice is a Chinese name for local use, and an English name for international use. Names are selected so as to project an image — an actual family name, for example, signals an established, reliable concern. Other names are invented to suggest a cosmopolitan, or a youthfully vigorous, or a fashionably up-to-the-minute image. Effective disguise obviously, had to be the first criterion: an image not dissimilar from that chosen by the companies was the second. The following is the list of pseudonyms in use.

- In Macau: *Songster, Irish Girl, Robinsons, Look Out*, and *Palace*.
- In Hong Kong: *Locks, Sign Writer, All Asia Wear*, and *Aviator*.

We adopt a similar procedure in disguising the names of the various suppliers and buyers.

3.2 Classification of the Database — Size and Distribution

In all, the database comprises just under a thousand pages of text assembled from the companies. Table 8 shows the distribution of the records, i.e. the

Table 8. Size of Database and Distribution of Records

Company (Pseudonym)	Location	No. of pages 1st Visit (1991)	No. of pages 2nd Visit (1993-4)
Songster	Macau	71	94
Irish Girl	Macau	66	208
Robinsons	Macau	131	
Look Out	Macau	13	17
Palace	Macau	61	
Locks	Hong Kong	83	
Sign Writer	Hong Kong	94	
All Asia Wear	Hong Kong	56	
Aviator	Hong Kong		84
		Total: 659	**Total: 319**

number of pages of documents by location, company, and time period of collection.

It quickly became apparent that each company had supplied a similar range of documents — each file includes faxes sent and received; official government and other forms, printed documents relating to the control of quality, promotional items, and some miscellaneous material. The documents that regularly recur in the files as a result of company business are of four distinct kinds:

- items related to advertising and promotion,
- official and quasi-official documents,
- texts resulting from self-regulatory business processes, internal to companies and
- incoming and outgoing faxes related to trade deals.

3.2.1 *Advertising and promotion*

These are very unevenly distributed. Senior personnel, asked on our second visit about ways in which they go about promoting products and obtaining new business, perceived the question as criticism of their practice: they believed they should do more about promotion — but the pace and pressure of work never seemed to allow them time. Standard promotional letters, often accompanied by illustrated brochures, were sometimes, they told us, mailed to prospective customers, but in general senior personnel felt that the promotion of trade was the responsibility of governments, and, at the company level, was most effectively accomplished by personal contact, at meetings or at trade fairs. The database contains some correspondence relating to such arrangements.

The exception to this was *Sign Writer*, an international company having its regional head office in Hong Kong, where much attention was paid to advertising of their sophisticated and easily copied product, and promotional materials constitute much of the contents of that file. Their advertisements were inserted regularly in trade journals. Our attention was particularly drawn to recent articles in which the company's products were favourably mentioned — a very effective form of publicity. In this competitive market however, advertising is generally and sensibly seen by small companies as of limited value, and heavy pressure of work on individuals reduces the time available for promotion.

3.2.2 *Records of government control*

Official and quasi-official forms are included in all the files. They are the means by which the governments of Hong Kong and Macau exert control over imports and exports and protect legitimate interests, including, of course, their own. English is the language regularly in use but others are not excluded. Regulation, development and control of international trade procedures are encoded in formal English, comprehension of which is assumed. The arrangement of the documents is designed for economy of space rather than ease of use; as in other official documents, the small print is designed to protect conflicting interests and is ignored by the users. Completing the forms is a task that falls (except in the smallest companies) to shipping clerks, who find it tedious, difficult, and repetitive. For each consignment despatched, the following documents must be assembled and completed, and copies forwarded to the receiver, who must produce them in order to take delivery of the goods.

- Bill of Lading
- Certificate of Origin
- Packing List
- Export License
- Invoice

There is no pressure for the sort of revision of format that might ease and speed completion. On the contrary, forms employed by buyers to ensure that quality is controlled by a random sampling of products resemble government forms in that they are economical of space, formal in expression, and appear difficult to use. These forms reflect the organisation of the task, i.e., they are categorised by commodity. Inspectors working for the buyer examine a random selection of products and check each against exhaustive lists of features of material, manufacture, finish and packing — regularly 50 to 60 items in all. They then have to make an overall assessment of acceptability of the product. Features not visibly apparent (for example the wearing quality of fabric) are frequently required by the buyer to be subjected to testing by government-operated laboratories. Documents by means of which quality is monitored in the buyers' interests are again in English, and are retained for reference.

3.2.3 *Self-regulation in the companies*

Items in this category provide evidence of a developing consciousness in the industry of a need to regulate its own practices. Some are simply traces that remain of company routines — we have lists of employees, samples of leave application forms, a notice of removal to other premises. Some are, however, ambitious, deliberate attempts to routinise good practice and to set new standards. The director of *Palace* provided a standardised Packing List in four languages, designed for use in his own company. Another company, *Look Out*, designed for its own use a Standard Letter of Guarantee. *Irish Girl* made available an ambitious marketing plan for the company's development. One English buyer regularly copied to its major supplier in Macau records of the company meetings at which the progress of current deals was subjected to critical review. More ambitious attempts at regulation came from powerful European buyers, who believe, almost certainly rightly, that they are in a position to impose their preferred forms of organisation on their suppliers. From one of these, *Songster* received a lengthy document in which an attempt was made to standardise, in five languages, the care instructions to be sewn inside garments. The same company provided with us a document, having government authority, regulating the condition of use of the *Woolmark* label. A standard letter from another buyer, couched in authoritative terms, declared its intention of ceasing to trade with any company shown to be involved in the use of gifts or inducements. At intervals, suppliers receive from buyers new sets of regulations governing packaging and shipment. To those working in the companies, it must seem that the conditions of international trade become all the time more stringent, and compliance with regulations more difficult, for businesses employing few, already pressured, senior personnel.

3.2.4 *Incoming and outgoing faxes*

These make up the most substantial part of the files of material already obtained during the first series of visits (1991) and were much extended as a result of the second series. Company personnel have no doubt that these represent the actual work in which they are engaged — the processes of regulation and financing are of course necessary, but they are contingent.

If factories *run on talk*, it can be said that *international trade business runs on fax*. The exchange of faxed correspondence is the means by which deals are initiated, and the often lengthy processes of enquiry, negotiation, monitoring and completion are accomplished.

Given our purposes and interest, faxed communication occupies a position of centrality. The use of English as an international language makes the process possible, and the use of faxed transmission has heavily reinforced the dominance of English. Faxes are kept in companies for their own purposes. They allow the details of successive negotiations of a contract, for example, to be available for reference, and they ensure that claims on the part of a buyer for a discounted price can be evaluated. They are central to our enquiry.

Independent of their primary function, they provide the means by which the micro-fabric of international trade processes can be the subject of investigation, and examples of particular deals can be reconstructed. Of those two activities, the first occupies part of the remainder of this chapter, and the second is the basis of the case studies in Chapter 4; the texts themselves are illustrated, contextualised, and made the subject of comment in Chapter 5.

3.3 Communication by Faxed Correspondence

3.3.1 *A preferred means of business communication*

Within a decade, faxed transmission has become the accepted way of doing international business. This circumstance, in relation to the international business community, the reasons for it, and its far-reaching implications, have been recently and persuasively argued by James (1995) in the following terms:

> " ... The speed with which fax machines have entered our lives is breathtaking. Several factors account for this. First, telecommunications technology is expanding globally at a lightning pace. Satellite transponders and telephone lines now reach even the most remote village. Second, fax equipment and transmission are affordable for many, in business and even in homes. Fax transmissions cost less than postage, at least compared with domestic mail. Third, graphic designs and Asian language script

> and ideograms transmit as easily as typeface. Handwriting and drawings can be clearly transmitted. .... Speed of delivery substantially enhances productivity. Efficiency experts have long pointed out that productivity is improved if you attend to a task immediately rather than put it off ..." (James 1995: 2)

In the garment and textile trade, speed is not the only advantage of fax technology. Fax allows the transmission not only of drawings and diagrams, but of photocopies of fabric itself, clearly indicative of texture, seaming, button-holes, eyelets and other details of garment construction and finish. Fax, unlike telephone communication, does not require calculation of time zones; it provides a written record. Perhaps most importantly, given that most users are employing their second language, it is much less vulnerable to failures of immediate comprehension and subsequent recall than is the use of the telephone. Accurate production of the sounds of English, and immediate comprehension of the spoken word are the very skills most difficult for users of English as a second language to acquire, and those in which they typically feel least secure. Where telephoned communication is used for any except the simplest messages, it has rapidly become established practice to send a summary of what was agreed upon in the conversation by fax, and expect faxed assent to its accuracy.

3.3.2 *International trade communication in English: Illustrative examples*

There is of necessity a time-lag between the development and use of a technology and the widespread availability of training in its use. Virtually nobody employed in the companies has received, before taking up employment, any systematic instruction in what has rapidly become the central activity of the merchandiser's working day, and the means by which the mediating role of the occupation is accomplished. Literacy in English is, supposedly, enough. It is for fax users themselves to develop, independent of instruction, the skills of using this mode of transmission to its best advantage, and of interpreting the faxed messages they receive.

It is predictable in these circumstances that a distinct and describable variety of English should emerge from their practice, and that it should be, at present, no more than partially stable. It is possible to identify and even to account for, some of its emerging characteristics, but there are differences between the usage of companies, of individuals, and even between the usage of the same individual at different times. Of the texts classified above (in Sec. 3.2.1), faxes have central importance, and for that reason, examples are included and some of those characteristics examined. Further, more extended, and more fully contextualised examples will be found at Chapter 5.

The first example was received by a Hong Kong company, *Locks*, from a Spanish buyer with which they have a business relationship of some standing. It should be said that this text is more obviously than most, the result of English imperfectly learnt. It illustrates some common features of the variety, and clearly indicates the actual difficulty of the comprehension tasks merchandisers undertake.

> **REFERENCE L/C WE ALRADY OPEN SINCE JANUARY 15th, AT MOMENT WE DO NOT HAVE L/C NUMBER BECOUSE BANKS IN SPAIN ARE TO SLOW,FOR THEY INFORM US THAT L/C IN H.K. DOLLARS IS NOT POSSIBLE ANY MORE IN SPAIN, WE DECIDE WITH OUT YOUR APROVALL TO DIVIDED ENTER 7.79 HK/USD 54,515.92 I DO NOT KNOW IF THIS RATE IS WORKABLE AT THIS MOMENT IF NOT I TAKE THIS DESICION IN YOUR VACATIONS IN ORDER TO SAVE TIME WAITING FOR YOU, PLEASE TRANSMIT YOUR PRO FORMA INVOICE IN ORDER TO AMENDED IF IS NECESARY.**

Comprehension and use of a communication like this requires a number of assumptions in the recipient. They may be verbalised as follows: Spelling and other errors are to be ignored, provided the reader recognises the meaning intended. Past tense endings (in *-ed*) occur randomly, but since a date earlier than Feb. 11th (on which it was received) is mentioned, the message relates to a past set of circumstances. The reader expects several clues to a set of circumstances that extend to the limit the writer's ability to encode them. These include contextual information, for example, that a Letter of Credit number is required for the next stage of the financing process, and in consequence, a missing number involves inconvenience and delay. There is an expectation, therefore, of apology and explanation. The blame is assigned by the buyer to the Spanish issuing bank — no longer, by his account, willing, or possibly able, to operate using Hong Kong currency. An amendment to the Letter of Credit so as to secure payment in US dollars has been made by the buyer, using information available locally about the current rate of exchange. This elliptical and unclear English relies very heavily on shared contextual knowledge.

The second example illustrates the unsettled and unstable character of faxed English, and demonstrates that it is not to be identified with the imperfectly learned English of second language users, although this may be an additional complicating factor. Some of them have a degree of control of the language that allows a choice to be made of a more or less close approximation to the Standard. They may, as the sender of the following faxes does, experiment with the best way to use faxes — and by the *best*, we mean the least expensive. There follow excerpts from two faxes, despatched by the same buyer (in Thailand) to the same Macau supplier, within a few weeks of each other:

> **22nd Oct.**
> **Buyr wl adv sz/col b/d whn recvg ur aprvl spl pls adv whn ready, so tht v cn cfm to our buyr Sz spec was snt to u b/4 w/sketch**
>
> **29th Nov.**
> **Enclosed please find balance original colour swatch in putty and main/care labels for the bove mentioned style .**

The second message approximates to Standard business usage, though it still requires knowledge of the context for its interpretation. The first is so elliptical as to require extensive paraphrase. Omissions must be supplied at each of two levels; first, the missing parts of heavily abbreviated words. This produces:

> **Buyer will advise size/colour (b/d) when receiving your approval sample please advise when ready so that we can confirm to our buyer. Size specification was sent to you before with sketch.**

There is then a *second* set of omissions to be supplied, and here the dependency of contextual information is such that it is not possible to offer more than a *best guess* at what is intended: These insertions are italicised:

> ***Our* Buyer will advise *you of the* size *and* colour (b/d) *required* when receiving your approval sample. Please advise *us* when *you are* ready, so that we can confirm *these details* to our buyer. *The* size specification was sent to you *earlier* with *an accompanying* sketch.**

Comparison between the elliptical original and the expanded version demonstrates that the omissions are principled, not random. Comprehension demands correct inference based on previous knowledge, breadth of detailed information, and immediacy of recall.

Two additional examples follow, both produced by merchandisers in Macau/ Hong Kong-based companies, and which are illustrative of the abbreviated and elliptical variety in use by suppliers and buyers alike. The excerpts selected are part of the routine monitoring of the production of a jacket. The question at issue is the exact position of a label on two styles currently in production. Full size sketches, faxed earlier, failed to resolve the uncertainty and allow production to go ahead. This is the next fax in the sequence:

> **AA RE PT 1 X NTD N WL PUT C.C. LBL AS YR SKETCH X BUT PLS ADV WHETHER C.C. LBL FOR" JORDACHE" LBL IS SEWN AS OLD METHOD UNDER CENTRE BACK NECK OR AS NEW METHOD UNDER MAIN LBL X**
>
> **BB RE PT 2 X SINCE 9/26 IS NOT AVAILB X WUD U PLS CONSIDER ON 9/25 OR 9/27 X PLS ADV TKS**
>
> **CC RE PT 5 PLS CFM IF IT CAN B FR PRODTN X TKS RGDS**

Again, the faxed English is characterised by abbreviation of words, and the omission of any reference to information which is assumed to be in possession of the reader and to be immediately recalled. It can be reconstructed as follows:

> **AA Regarding your point 1 — *that is* noted and we *will* put *in* the C.C. label *in accordance with* your sketch. But please advise us whether the C.C. label for the garments *having the* Jordache label should be sewn in *according to* the old method, under the centre of the back of the neck, or *according to* the new method, below the main label.**
>
> **BB *Regarding your* point 2: since 26th September *is* not available *for the proposed meeting*, would you please consider either the 25th September or the 27th September? Please advise us *of your decision*. Thanks**
>
> **CC Regarding your point 5 — please confirm if the order *to which this correspondence* relates *can be authorised* for production. Thanks. Regards.**

The second point, identified by the double uppercase BB, relates to another matter. There is tacit understanding among users that a fax will usually serve as the vehicle for a number of messages, not related to each other except in the general sense of being concerns for both the sender and the receiver. The assumption is that the fax will be dealt with immediately, each message receiving whatever attention is sufficient and/or action is appropriate before the receiver goes on to the next. Continuity or contrast among different topics is not expected. The layout of the page and the identification of message boundaries by letter or number are signals of the sort of topic change to be paraphrased by "*On a different topic* ..." or "*now to another matter* ...".

The questions posed in this fourth example result from the receipt of correspondence that leaves critically important information impossible to interpret with any certainty. It illustrates not so much the limitations of faxed English, but the way in which merchandisers handle serious ambiguity. The sender of the fax cited below locates the topic of this fax in the previous correspondence, identifies the deal by reference to the garment, and the supposed destination of the order. Then there is clearly information that his company, as the supplier, does not have, and so indicates the alternatives at each salient point, only one of which must be correct. This fax virtually compels an explicit and informative answer.

RE CUSTOMER ORDER NO 042/2309/1601/60 1 ORDER NO 10-064 1000

PCS , OF BOY'S PULLOVER TO FRANCE
WE HAVE RECEIVED YOUR L/C , AND HAVE THE FOLLOWING DETAILS THAT WE ARE NOT CLEAR:-

A FINAL DESTINATION TO FRANCE OR NOT

E SHIPMENT BY AIR OR SEA

C IF MAIL BY AIR , THE AIRWAY BILL'SCONSIGNEE SHOULD READ BANKER'S NAME OR CLIENT'S NAME

D CAT 68 & 5 -WAITING YOUR REPLY (RE : F-5979)
BEST REGARD

The reference here to some "details" saves the face of the buyer by minimising he importance of the ambiguities in the earlier correspondence. In fact, these are not in any sense questions about details, they relate to critically important information without which the next stage of a nearly completed deal cannot possibly proceed. Senders of faxes are not always correct in their estimate of the receivers' ability to supply information, but receivers have in place strategies for identifying and obtaining what is missing.

3.4 An Interim Summary

Some provisional inferences and conclusions are appropriate at this point and can be summarised as follows: A text-based study of the communicative processes involved in trade deals is practicable, and fully supports the assertion that they are fundamental and indispensable to lives and livelihoods dependent on trade; the role of intermediaries between and among the buyer and the supplier, the exercise of control by governments, and the financing of trade procedures by banks, is undertaken collectively by innumerable small concerns, and individually by merchandisers employed in them. The internalised knowledge and skills involved are not usually articulated and no more than partially institutionalised in educational systems, and get little explicit recognition. It is however possible to articulate them; merchandisers (individually or collectively) require a knowledge of whatever *lingua franca* is common to buyer and seller, which means, in contemporary conditions, of English; this knowledge may fall well short of so difficult an attainment as an even bilingualism, and may not include an even development of the skills of speaking and writing. Extensive knowledge of trade proceedings is crucial; equally important is the ability to use it in the interpretation of often deviant texts.

Chapter 4

Five Case Studies

The case studies that follow narrow our focus to the consideration of selected, particular deals, reconstructed using the documents described in the preceding chapter. Our intention is that these text-based narratives shall provide some familiarity with business as it is conducted in the companies, with the pace, the pressure and the variety of the transactions which, in the aggregate, constitute international trade. The narratives are also intended to show why and how all stages of production and trade in textiles and garments are dependent on a continuous flow of information between buyer and supplier. While the cases are based on data from Hong Kong and Macau, and drawn from the textile and garment industry, they are certainly typical, perhaps with minor modifications, for production and trade throughout Asia, where English is not the first language.

The contents of the extended database are currently stored as part of the New Zealand Social Research Data Archive at Massey University, and can be accessed on the Internet. A sample of the data on which the first of the case studies is based (transcribed, and with those changes or omissions only when they are necessary to protect the anonymity of the informants) will be found in the Appendix, and relates to the first of these case studies.

The records available represent most (but not all) of the elements of a complete deal. The initial enquiry and the detailed summary of the terms agreed upon (but not a formal contract) are included, as is the process of monitoring production, the control of quality, the modifications in response to requests by the buyer, the completion of the order, packing and shipment.

These elements are well described by the term preferred by Fairclough (1993), following Levinson (1983) as *a structured sequence of action*. They are defined by their content rather than by linguistic features. The boundaries between stages are not rigid. So long as the manufacturing process continues, and the merchandisers are prepared to negotiate, there is the possibility of modifications to what was earlier agreed upon.

4.1 Yachtsman Jersey 3

The source of information

Though this first reasonably complete file allows for the reconstruction of most of the sequence, there are some notable omissions. Copies of Letters of Credit were not made available in this case. Nor were there copies of the documentation required in addition to the Inspection Certificate, at the point where goods are shipped — Certificate of Origin, Export License, Packing List, and Bill of Lading.

The relations between the merchandisers are, as a rule, those of easy equality; they regularly use first names (in English) and conclude faxes with expressions of regard and good wishes. Neither is in a *permanently* advantaged position relative to the other. At the outset, a potential buyer is in the more powerful negotiating position, but the balance shifts in favour of the supplier once agreement on a deal is reached. After that, the two parties each have an interest in its successful completion, and they bargain on nearly equal terms. The supplier gives way rather easily on two occasions in the course of this deal because her priority is to extend the company's range rather than to maximise profit on a limited deal. The language used is direct to the point of abruptness. A strong sense is communicated of there being no time for elaboration — or even for writing in full what can be abbreviated.

This deal is negotiated between a Macau supplier, which we call *Look Out*, and a French buyer with a buying office located in Hong Kong. The subject of the deal is a single product, a striped cotton pullover. There is a well-established relation between buyer and supplier, and the participants, Catherine, in *Look*

Out, and Cindy and her colleague Heidi in Hong Kong are, at least in their working roles, well-known to each other.

In choosing *Yachtsman Jersey 3* as an alternative to the actual trade name we have tried to preserve the original image of casualness, and the association with sport, youth, light-heartedness, perhaps even luck. The deal was small in scale — the total number of garments packed and despatched was just under a thousand. The transaction went through quite quickly — between June and early November — and was unusually straightforward. There were problems of course, but they were rapidly identified and resolved by an alert and experienced merchandiser in the supplier's office, and her senior position allowed her to take the responsibility involved in treating the deal as a loss leader. Sportswear was a new venture for her company and potentially highly profitable, but only if the buyer could be thoroughly pleased and eager to continue and extend trading in this and similar lines.

A reconstruction of the deal: Towards confirmation of an order

The deal starts when the buyers select for attention *Yachtsman Jersey 3*, one of several products in a list of items faxed to them from *Look Out* in Macau. Within a month of receipt of this information, the buyers ask the supplier for samples of *Yachtsman Jersey 3*. This request is not included in the records and may well have been telephoned. The buyers' faxed comments, quoted below in full (additional explanatory notes are italicised) on the sample dated 16th June, are favourable, and effectively set the deal in motion.

Re: Yachtsman Jersey 3

The sent counter sample was rcvd + comments as below:-

– style : ok

– weight : We prefer to keep the weight as yr smpl 310gm/m2 I/O original in 280 gm/m2 for production.

– collar & cuff : We want the collar & cuff with spandex not as yr smpl.

– measurement : 1) ok for the cut & sewn on sleeve & bottom but pls modify the measurement as follows:-

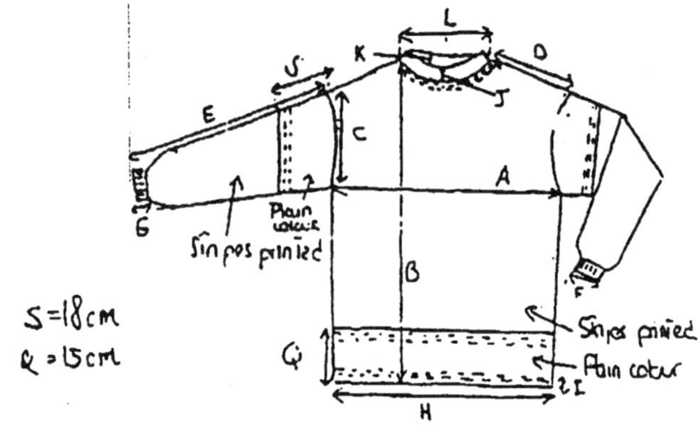

2) other measurement are ok.
– We would like an half-moon back as next page.

Merchandisers know that garments are not available from stock, but are made to order, so that details of manufacture and production, like time schedule and price, are subject to negotiation. The preferences of buyers, based on their assessment of their own retail market, can be accommodated. The reply by the buyer, on behalf of the French company, approves the overall style and design, but she asks for an elasticised cuff, some modification of the measurements, and a change to the design of the upper back of the garment. She wants a second sample that takes into account these requirements, and notification of a date by which it can be expected. Samples are expensive for a supplier to produce, and some objection might be anticipated, but there is none. Two days later, the supplier in Macau receives additional instruction from the Hong Kong buying office, which has been in touch with the head office in France. A preference has been expressed for a different fabric from that used in the original sample — one with a harder, firmer texture — perhaps more in keeping with the outdoor image which the garment is intended to project. This will, it is assumed, involve additional processing and a consequent increase in cost. Before sending her an almost immediate reply, the Macau supplier, having checked with the factory where the production takes place, finds out that, as it stands, this requirement cannot be met. Stone-washing, the finish preferred by the buyer, cannot be applied without damage to the striped cotton fabric. There is however an alternative — a process called *heavy sand-wash*. The change could be made at a higher additional cost. A sample could be available within a few days if the alternative were acceptable to the buyer. Again, there may have been telephone calls of which we have no record, agreeing to this suggestion, and acknowledging receipt of the sample. A month elapses before the Macau supplier sends details of what can be offered, including fabric weight and constituents, garment construction and finish, size range, price, EEC Quota Category, mode of payment, and arrangements for shipment.

Acceptance of the offer, which would imply agreement to a contract and initiate production, is not however immediate. A fax from Hong Kong on 21st July, commenting on the most recent sample, requires further modifications, of which the most substantial is that those parts of the garment which are not striped, but are made in a solid colour, should be navy blue rather than white. The buyer likes the heavy sand-washed finish. There is a reminder to Catherine that these changes must be implemented in the bulk production — implying that the contract is now to be regarded as agreed and production can begin.

Monitoring the manufacturing process

Although additional modifications may still be requested, having a confirmed order puts the supplier, in principle at least, in a marginally stronger bargaining position. In this case, that advantage is moderated, however, by some anxiety on the merchandiser's part that this deal, the first of its kind in an area of potentially high profit, shall be an unqualified success from the buyer's standpoint. The merchandiser in Macau, acting on the part of the manufacturer, immediately confirms the terms and conditions of the agreement, and asks her Hong Kong counterpart to take into account an error for which she holds the factory responsible, in the terms that follow.

RE: SPOT MEN KNIT – Yachtsman Jersey 3

ReYr Fax 8170 DD 22/7/93.
HV CHKD W/Factory AND CFMD the fllwg:-
– FAB QLTY : 100% cotton French RIB, 320 g/m2 (after print & wash).
– QTIES : 1,000 PCS in one colorway.
– PX : USD 11.30/PC (Pls note TT 0/quoted PX is based on SMPL I.E. the plain color part is to be white. Hever, since YR client RQSTD the plain color part to be navy,

		XTRA costs is involved. But since this is the 1st order W/spot men knit, V SHLL not increase the PX).
– SHPT	**:**	**5/11/93.**
– Quota	**:**	**E.E.C. 4 to France**
– MK-UP	**:**	**Normal MK-UP. XTRA accessories such as woven LBL + Hang tag will be subjt to XTRA charges.**
– TERMS	**:**	**FOB(+Quota) HONG KONG ; L/C at sight.**

The sample sent initially was made up in a heavier, and therefore a better quality and more expensive fabric than the one tested and made the basis of agreement. This error, she says, will be rectified at the stage of bulk production. She does not draw attention to what is obvious to both parties — that it is to the advantage of the supplier to use the less expensive fabric. If a deviation from the terms agreed were first noticed by the *buyer*, there would be grounds for the negotiation of a discounted price.

A telephone conversation follows, referred to, and its terms recorded, in a fax dated 27th July. The heavier fabric was the one seen by the buyer: the price was accepted in the belief that the fabric that was seen would be the one used in manufacture. The merchandiser, on behalf of the supplier, is prepared to make a concession, involving a cost to her company, in the longer term interest.

Another discrepancy comes to light, potentially more troublesome, and is the subject of a fax (on 5th August) from Macau. It is the merchandiser acting for the supplier who identifies the problem, and checks the supplier's legal position with the authorities in Macau before faxing Hong Kong. If, as the buyer in France requests, these goods are shipped under EEC Category 5, and not, as has been assumed hitherto, under Category 4, there will have to be an increase in the price. The Hong Kong buyer must ensure that her Hong Kong Buying Office draws this to the attention of the head office in France, where the decision about the choice of Category must be made — and made quickly, since the packing and shipping schedules are already in place, and are very tight. By 9th August, a compromise has been agreed. There will be shipment on the terms requested by the buyer, and an increase of US 40 cents on each garment — an increase which, as the supplier points out, does not represent the whole of the additional cost to the supplier, but brings the total cost to USD11.70. Brief faxes from Hong Kong indicate approval of specific features of the materials used in manufacture and production. On the 14th of October, the Macau supplier receives comments from the head office in France, relayed through the Hong Kong Buying Office, on the re-production samples. There are, even at this late stage, requests for adjustments to be made to measurements and stitching.

Inspection, packing, shipping

There is, then, silence — until 4th November, when the supplier, in response to a request from Hong Kong, faxes a report of her own inspection, not of the completed garments (that has to be the responsibility of the buyer), but of the details of their labelling and packing. By this time, the Macau company is right up against the deadline for shipping. All that is needed is the immediate despatch from Hong Kong of an Inspection Certificate. She requires this document to reserve shipping space - and the deadline for reservation is the following day. That Inspection Certificate, protecting the buyer's right to seek compensation for any deviation from the terms agreed, is the final item in the faxed sequence.

4.2 A Million Dollar Deal in Jeans

The file and its source

This case study is based on one of a number of very substantial files provided by the company we call *Robinsons*. The buyer in this deal, coded by the company *LH/39* to distinguish it from the many deals currently at different stages of development, is a Canadian company, and the intention is that the goods shall, after arrival in Vancouver, be distributed among retail outlets in several major Canadian cites. The deal is negotiated through an agent, acting for the Canadian buyer, and based in Thailand. *Robinsons* make jeans in a variety of fabrics and designs for world wide export. The processes of garment manufacture, the packing and shipping and all the communication and documentation associated with the business, take place in a flatted factory in the crowded centre of peninsular Macau. The company has an office in Laos. The Chinese director and owner of the family business, describes the concern modestly as of "medium size". He himself acts as the senior merchandiser, regularly receives most of the correspondence, and usually drafts the responses, only occasionally delegating this responsibility to a senior employee. His counterparts in Thailand are Ekanan and Somnuk. The file gives us access only to the intermediate and concluding stages of deal LH/39, but well illustrates the extent and complexity of the deals that Macau-based companies routinely undertake, and the meticulous attention to detail, sustained throughout the processes of manufacture, that international trade in textiles requires.

A substantial deal in progress

Order *LH/39* is for 12,500 pairs of jeans, in four colours and six sizes. The correspondence made available to us covers the period between October 1990 and the conclusion of the deal in the spring of 1991.

By 22nd October, the deal has already advanced to the point where the buyer has accepted a price of HKD45 per piece, based on the use of 100% cotton twill fabric, bringing the total value of the deal to almost one million HKD. *Robinsons* has already been able to secure agreement on size specifications, and has agreed to supply the samples which will be the basis for further decisions. A month later, on 21st November, a fax from Thailand confirms that the expected samples have been received, makes an enquiry — though not critically, simply as a matter of information — about the construction of the weave, and informs *Robinsons* of a number of decisions already taken by the buyer regarding the accessories that are to be supplied. (*Accessories* means all forms of fastening and labelling, and include the protective bags in which the garments are packed). Horn buttons are particularly required. *Robinsons* is asked to send samples to be retained in Thailand for later reference, and to forward results of laboratory tests of fabric.

The deal is evidently going well — but the fax sounds a note of warning about the general condition of trade in Canada —

Busines in Canada vy soft. All importers r offr vy low prx

Another deal that had at one time looked promising, and in which *Robinsons* had already invested some time and effort, looks as if it will come to nothing. There are no further references to this disappointment. Within a week, there is another fax from Thailand, with a sketch indicating exactly how the care label is to be attached to each garment. It seems that the construction of the fabric has by this stage been agreed upon without debate. Three colours have been approved for production, and *Robinsons* are asked to proceed with dyeing, and to send swatches of the dyed fabrics for reference. Care label samples are required, made according to the instructions already supplied, and photo-samples should be sent by early January. *Robinsons* is assured that the buyer is on the point of opening Letters of Credit, and that samples should be expected of the sort of *polybag* used for packing the garments.

A build-up of pressure on the supplier

The polybag arrives with an accompanying fax four days later. At this stage, the garment fastenings and labels receive detailed attention. The buyer has already approved the metal zip fastener submitted by *Robinsons* — but now wants *all* the fasteners dyed to match the fabrics. There is a request for confirmation that the horn buttons requested are actually available, and still no indication of the length of the fastener preferred by the buyer. A drawing is included with this fax, showing the exact position that the care label should occupy, and there is a request for confirmation that the Macau supplier has fully understood each of these instructions. On 25th December (evidently not a public holiday in Thailand, though the fax concludes with Christmas greetings), the agents for the buyer fax again. Results of the laboratory tests, asked for in October, duly arrived, and were passed on to the Canadian buyer. Now there is a query as to whether and when the photographic samples were sent. The buyer requires them on *that day* (someone has pencilled in an exclamation mark at this point). The size of the zip fastener should be six inches right across the size range. Contrary to custom, no hang-tags are needed. The buyer has agreed to shipment of the order in two consignments, one in June, and one in August of the coming year. *Robinsons* should immediately confirm the feasibility of those dates. The pressure is on.

Shifting the balance of power

A reply is sent, not on that day (a public holiday in Macau) but the next, and not over the director's signature, but over that of a senior employee. This may in itself be a signal that the supplier is, at this stage, with the deal well towards completion, prepared to exert some resistance to pressure. The photographic samples have *not* been sent: they will be speed-posted (not faxed) that day. Colour codes for the metal zip fasteners are submitted, as requested, for approval, but with a warning reservation. The technician in the supplier's employ advises against the buyer's expressed preference. Longer fasteners should, he says, be inserted into the larger sizes. Furthermore, *Robinsons* have requests to make of the buyer through his agent. They want a sample of the horn buttons and a breakdown of the colour and size assortment to be included in each of the two consignments. This is the point at which, with the deal well advanced towards completion, there is an evident shift in the balance of bargaining power in favour of the supplier.

The response is conciliatory. On 3rd January, a fax arrives with thanks for the photographic samples, together with approval of size specifications and acknowledgement of another change made by *Robinsons* on their own initiative, in the interests of good fit and good appearance. The details of the assortment required in each of the two consignments arrive within a few days, with approval for the remaining colour (putty) and — since the goods are for the Canadian retail market — a list in French and English of the colour terms to be used. The final form of the contract has yet, at this stage, to be received from the Canadian buyer. Letters of Credit are open, and inspection can now be arranged in the Laos Office of the Macau-based company. In advance of any comment from the buyer, *Robinsons* correct the French from *Fabrique a Laos* to *Fabrique au Laos*. (It is part of the conditions of the deal that the garments shall be labelled in this way rather than in accordance with their actual place of manufacture.) Additional zips are forwarded for the reference collection. Final approvals and instructions are faxed on 26th January. On 5th February, the Macau-based supplier are able to acknowledge receipt of the contract, to arrange for all accessories other than those associated with packing to be sent by mid-March, to ask for instructions about folding (since the size of the polybags is dependent on this) and to enquire whether the samples already supplied are approved for bulk production. Sketches showing exactly how garments are to be folded arrive on 8th February. *Robinsons* forward, in response to a request for careful checking of measurements, a detailed table of eight measurements for each of six sizes, with diagrams showing the exact position and measurement of pockets and belt loops.

Concerns for quality

There is an immediate response. Faults have been identified in the manufacture. There is single stitching where double stitching was agreed, pleats are not correctly set in, button-holes are mis-matched to buttons. All these critical comments are illustrated with diagrams, and *Robinsons* is asked to confirm that the comments have been received and clearly understood. The response, however, is that while the criticisms are indeed understood, the supplier is not prepared, at this stage of the deal, to comply without question. Single stitching was intentionally chosen, they say, to suit the fabric. Eyelets, not button-holes, are intended for use with the buttons. Does the buyer really want these changes? They can be made of course — but *Robinson* cannot guarantee that if they are, the appearance of the completed garments will be as good.

However, the Canadian buyer will not give way on the issue of single stitching, and — as is clear from a fax sent on 2nd April — the supplier is obliged to make the change. The question of button-holes or eyelets is more tricky, and must await discussion with the agent for the buyer. Further samples are required from *Robinsons* on 27th March, demonstrating the appearance of the fabric before and after washing. As a result, it is late March before inspection can actually be arranged.

The conclusion of the deal

By 1st April the deal is in its closing stages. A fax arrives from Thailand with details of the assortment to be included in each of the two consignments. Even at this stage, they notice differences in the colour of the fabric used in garments of different sizes and require correction of the discrepancy. The supplier is, at that late stage, still awaiting confirmation that the use of eyelets is acceptable to the buyer. A very long fax — nine pages — from Thailand on 8th April, confirms the arrangements for packing and shipment, including the design and labelling of the cartons in which the polybags are packed, only to be followed the next day by modifications of these arrangements, and a request for confirmation of the receipt of both. *Robinsons* comply with this request on 5th April — and, on the following day, is asked for confirmation of the status of the deal, required to make yet another change to the packing arrangements. In addition, the director of Robinsons is asked to meet a representative of the Canadian company in Bangkok in May. The supplier refuses this late request to change the packing schedule, since the change could be made only at the cost of a delay in delivery. Nor is the director willing to be in Bangkok for the meeting — he is due in Bangkok earlier, and he has appointments with other clients in May. Nor, according to this fax, can the last change of plan in respect of packing instructions be accommodated. A change initiated by *Robinsons* and not notified earlier, must be approved. A set of shipping advices completes the file on a deal that has been brought, not altogether easily, to a successful conclusion.

4.3 The Work Week of a Company Merchandiser

The source of the information

This case study is based on a selection from correspondence between the Macau-based company, *Songster*, and the Hong Kong buying office of a well-known international company, which also has buying offices in Singapore, Toronto and Panama. The correspondence was unusually frequent. Five days in May 1991 produced, even with a number of items missing from the collection, 26 items of correspondence between two merchandisers working for the respective companies. The first names used constantly in the correspondence — Bonnie, in Macau, and Nita, her counterpart in Hong Kong — have been retained in the account that follows.

The system of numbering items of correspondence used in Macau provides evidence of many missing items. What we have, however, is enough to offer some insight into that considerable part of a merchandiser's working day, which is occupied in writing or responding to faxed correspondence in English.

Monday

The week begins quietly for Bonnie, acting for the supplier, in Macau, with the receipt of two faxes. One is a cancellation of a meeting due to be held with a Japan-based licensee of the company. A delay in the despatch of orders is given as the reason for the change. This is not an urgent matter, and response can wait wait till the following day. The second fax is from Nita in the Hong Kong office.

There are in all eight matters requiring attention, each in connection with a different, current deal. Each assumes in the merchandiser an immediate recall of the details of each order. First, there is a piece of welcome news. A buyer has confirmed an order in connection with the *Boys'* trousers and blazers programme. (A *programme* refers to a range of garments intended for a specific market in various colours and sizes, comprising a single order) They want a mid-June despatch date, and since that is little more than a month ahead, work must proceed immediately. Information follows — presumably in answer to an enquiry in the previous week — that a missing document, in connection with the shipping of an order, was despatched by Federal Express on 13th May, and should, by the time she receives the fax, be already in her hands. Next she is reminded that an invoice is required in respect of another deal, and should be faxed to Hong Kong immediately. The next point refers to the supply of zip fasteners required for the completion of another programme. Three pages are enclosed with the fax, giving details of the sizes and colours of zips needed for production of the whole range of garments, and with it a reminder that this is no more than provisional information. The buyers may still change their minds about the quantities in each style and colour. The next point has to do with supplies of fabric for another programme, gives details of the expected despatch and arrival dates, and on the basis of these, asks for an anticipated date for the completion and delivery of the finished garments. The fifth item has to do with another deal again — one already well advanced; prices have been determined, and Nita expects to advise Bonnie of the availability of Letters of Credit soon. There is an update on the price of jeans, and a request for comment on a sample as soon as it is received. Point 6 informs that the thread to be used in manufacture of another item has been approved, and can be ordered. In conclusion, Nita acknowledges receipt and understanding of a number of items of information communicated by Bonnie, and explains her own reluctance to engage in correspondence about freight charges for a fabric shipment. She is not, she says, in possession of the documentation needed to support the claim, and in any case, negotiation of this sort is properly the responsibility of the licensee. The fax ends, as is customary between these two, with handwritten good wishes and expressions of regard. The fax comprises, as is usual, a demanding agenda of work, most, but not all, of which will be completed immediately, and some of which will be the subject of further correspondence.

Tuesday

The fax of the previous day's date is answered. Some items — four in all — need only to be acknowledged. Bonnie supplies details of the outstanding freight charges referred to, encloses for Nita's reference a copy of a debit note in support of her statement, and thanks her for her assistance. Until she has more details about the shipment of fabric, she cannot estimate a date of completion for the order. As for the collection of freight charges that Nita mentions in the later part of her fax, difficulties in this regard are nothing new, and she quotes an example.

On that day, Bonnie sends a fax to the Singapore office to acknowledge receipt of the information about cancellation of the Japan arrangements. A second fax to Singapore (copied to Hong Kong) requests assistance in getting licensees of the parent company to settle payment of freight charges promptly — and in support of it, eight debit statements are enclosed. Another fax comes in from Hong Kong, in which the first item is a repetition of information already arrived — that the thread submitted is acceptable. The second informs her of a change in an order — one that Nita believes will not cause Bonnie too much trouble, since the prototype sample of this order has not yet been approved. A faxed request sent on 16th May (and not included in our data collection) gets an answer — additional blazer buttons, needed for completion of an order, are on their way. There is a request from Hong Kong for information relating to an item identified as *Mexico Ranch Dungaree*. This is a matter of urgency, since there is already an estimated delivery date on the Panama order. Shipping arrangements for this last order are already in hand, and should be available on the 3rd June. Given a lead time for production of two months, 3rd August should be the completion date, and on behalf of the buyer, Nita will assume the practicability of her supplier meeting this deadline unless she is informed that such a schedule is *not* possible. There is a problem for Bonnie in relation to the trim required on an order having the code name *Marine Fat Pant* — Nita undertakes to pursue this on her behalf. Before the end of Tuesday, Bonnie receives a fax from a senior employee in the Singapore office, whose responsibility is to secure quality assurance in respect of products. He is generally dissatisfied with current standards. His instruction is that more care is needed at every stage of garment production, and in particular, that the degree of shrinkage in washable garments should be more consistent, and more closely controlled. Larger samples than before should be tested, and the design of patterns should allow for shrinkage of material.

Wednesday

A fax from Hong Kong includes a number of items. Another batch of thread has been approved for purchase. There is a response to a fax referred to by number (and not made available) which has to do with a query in respect of the Panama buyer. Nita will pursue this, and advise Bonnie. She attempts to resolve a confusing change of code name for a garment: an item formerly referred to as *Sienna pant* has been replaced by a similar one, with a code name formerly, but not recently, in use — *hacking pant.* The difficulty is recognised: Bonnie, as the recipient, is asked to confirm her understanding. Nita undertakes to do what she can to secure immediate payment of the outstanding freight charges, to find out details of a missing consignment of fabric, and to explain to the Panama buyer the difficulties experienced in Macau over the fabric shipment. Nita responds in her next point to an earlier fax (again not included in our collection). Evidently, Bonnie was aware that some of the licensees were left with stock of surplus fabric: Nita will look into the matter, and keep Bonnie informed. There is a delivery schedule for the trimming required to complete the order for helmets in the *Boys* range. An acknowledgement of receipt is needed from Bonnie. There is more about the problem of label differences in the *Mexico* order. Bonnie said "there are 2 diff ways of care instruction" but Nita is unsure what this means, and asks for further explanation.

That Wednesday Bonnie sends out several faxes. She acknowledges, without comment, the criticisms about the shrinkage of fabric. She confirms in writing the substance of an earlier telephoned query about the availability of good quality garments from factory stock. There are, she says, none at all. Any that might still be available are seconds. There is no record of any pursuit of this matter. She replies to the most recent fax from Nita, noting some points made, and agreeing that if *Sienna pant* is to be replaced by *hacking pant,* she will ensure that pre-made pockets and waist-bands are reserved for use with this garment. No answer can be given about a delivery date until a colleague, at present on leave from the office, returns on the 23rd of that month. She would like to have fabric swatches before selecting and reserving zip fasteners for use, and she needs to know whether these items should be laboratory-tested.

A fax from Singapore informs Macau that inspection certificates have been despatched by courier in respect of an invoice, and requires that in future suppliers must supply *four* copies of any invoice, in addition to a cargo receipt. In Hong Kong, a fax sent to Hong Kong from Canada is forwarded for information, saying that a package of helmet buttons is on its way by Federal Express. That package contains all the remaining buttons, and the sender just hopes there will be enough.

Thursday

Only some of at least ten faxes sent from Macau on this busy day are included in our data collection. Some are routine exchanges of information. Bonnie sends the Hong Kong address of her Macau-based company to the Head Office of the international company, and copies the fax to Nita. Details of a deal, completed in March, go to the Head Office, again with a copy to Hong Kong. Bonnie pursues the matter of delayed payment on that deal. All the relevant documents were, she says, despatched in April, and she needs the assistance of the Hong Kong agent in getting settlement of the account. One of the set of documents is copied for inclusion with this fax.

Bonnie acknowledges receipt of the previous day's fax, and indicates that she has noted each point made. There is another matter — the subject of a troubled fax to Nita. According to their Macau forwarder, eight cartons of fabric are due to arrive in Hong Kong the following day — Friday 20th May. None of the documents that have to be produced for the cargo to be cleared through Customs are available in Macau. Worse still, Bonnie has no idea what programme the fabric might be intended for. She asks for Nita's assistance in getting this information and, more immediately, in getting the Hong Kong shippers to send a set of documents, so the goods can be cleared through Customs. This fax is faintly overwritten, probably by Bonnie, after receiving a response later that day, or as a result of a telephone call, to the effect that all this was simply a mistake on the part of the shipping forwarder, and could have been disregarded altogether — but in the meantime it is a matter for anxiety and cannot be allowed to go unresolved.

A number of faxes unrelated to this issue come in during the day. One is from Singapore, to ask that samples of zip fasteners be tested for colour fastness. Two arrive from Nita — but her system for keeping track of faxes by means of reference numbers does not indicate the order of their arrival. One is a price-table for Bonnie's reference for the item coded *CCG6 Chambray*. It contains news of when several items of information can be expected. Nita tried, as she promised, to resolve the matter of late payment of freight charges — but without success. Canadian companies, she explains, try to arrange for freight charges to be pre-paid by their suppliers, and provided this is done, it is implied, payments can be made promptly. Where manufacturers are *not* willing to comply with this arrangement, costs have to be met in Macau and later reimbursed. In that event, delays are unavoidable. Another fax from Nita, sent on the same day, includes a table showing recent revisions to a deal in progress, tabulated by size and colour. There is confirmation of a recent telephone call in which it was agreed that *Mexico Ranch Dungarees* could not, after all, be made in Macau, since there was no access to machines designed to stitch the heavy fabric required in their manufacture. Nita asks for acknowledgement of receipt of samples; explains a delay in forwarding fabric for the *Panama* order (on which tests are needed to ensure it meets U.S. standards for shrink-resistance), and agrees to send material for the manufacture of *Sienna pant.* She has a further set of requests in yet another fax. She needs prices on four items and suggests at this point, in response to the query about the cartons of unidentified fabric, that Bonnie should check with the Macau forwarder who was the source of the information. It is to be assumed that Bonnie did so, either then, or on her own initiative, earlier, and that the handwritten note was either a note of the call or a reminder to fax as a result of it. Finally, Bonnie received from Nita a copy of a fax sent to her from the Singapore office, identifying revised quantities of *Classic pant* and *America pant*. Some colours are to be deleted from the range.

Friday

Again, the first of the day's faxes sent to Hong Kong. Only one item seems to trouble Bonnie. Most of the items are simply noted, or there is agreement to send the information or the samples required. However, the prospect of continuing to pay freight charges from Canada, and to await reimbursement after an indefinite interval, is another matter. Bonnie points out that this is a new and very unwelcome item of expenditure and that the sums involved are large.

A fax goes to Singapore acknowledging request for the sample of zip fasteners and receipt of a document sent from Singapore only that day. The document is an audit summary, relating to her Macau company, showing factory performance between January and April of that year. The measure employed is the percentage of goods randomly tested by the buyer, and found to be faulty, and the results seem to indicate a high, and steadily rising, level of performance, and in no way confirm the dissatisfaction with current standards expressed in the fax she received on the previous Tuesday. Most of the items in a fax from Hong Kong are straightforward acknowledgements. She does however address the issue of freight charges. It seems she has again been in touch with the Canadian company, who have assured her that if the suppliers they depend on do not co-operate over the freight charges, then they are powerless — they do, however, promise immediate reimbursement of charges paid in Macau. Given Bonnie's experience of delays in the settlement of accounts, it is not likely that this news brings her week to a very satisfactory conclusion.

Summary

It is easy to see why merchandisers find their work stressful: standards expected in production become steadily more stringent as business becomes increasingly competitive; dilatory buyers create extreme anxiety in small scale businesses dependent on banks for trade finance. The quantity and diversity of information exchanged is very large, and requires those who send and receive it to be always alert, to distinguish routine items from potential problems requiring to be identified and, if at all possible, resolved. There is constant pressure to expedite and complete deals quickly. It is noticeable that the two women, employed respectively by the supplier and the buyer of textiles, do not see themselves as representing opposed interests; on the contrary, they work collaboratively in the interests of successful dealing.

Merchandisers are so entirely immersed in the details of whatever business is their current preoccupation that the immediate recall of the context is not difficult. That recall is simply a part of their expertise. Some difficulties are associated with their way of working, which could, in principle, be reduced. Much of what that is important is retained in the memory of experienced merchandisers and nowhere else, so that in the absence of one of them, matters regarded as her responsibility cannot be forwarded, and have to await her return. There is no sifting or marking out of what is intended to be kept for reference from what is of immediate, but transient, importance.

4.4 Failure

In the garment and textile trade, successful outcomes are the norm. The case that follows is untypical, in that strenuous effort is expended, but eventually, the deal falls through just when it looks as if it may succeed against the odds. The participants in this case are more numerous, and the lines of communication longer than usual. The main protagonists are Lenny, a merchandiser for the Norwegian-owned, Hong Kong-based company, *Aviator*, which is, in this deal, the supplier. Lenny's position is unusual in that his inexperience makes him dependent for information and advice on his superior, Elvor, with whom he maintains frequent communication. The buyer, Stephen, works for a company called *EasternTex, and* acts in this deal on behalf of a Japanese client not named in the correspondence. It becomes apparent only at a late stage that the Japanese client is new, that the approach to *Aviator* on his behalf has been made on the recommendation of *EasternTex*, and that his patronage is potentially valuable to both companies.

The initial enquiries

In August 1991, when this correspondence begins, it is only one of several matters occupying Lenny's attention in *Aviator*, chief among them a deal in progress with a new customer, and arrangements for a stand to be set up for the international company at an approaching trade fair. Lenny sends a fax to two of his Norwegian colleagues, which begins informally with the hope that they have enjoyed the summer holidays from which they have just returned, before turning to items of business. He has recently received enquiries from two companies. No more is heard in the correspondence of one: the other is the prospective Japanese buyer. He was able to make only a provisional response immediately on receipt of the enquiry because he had no up-to-date price lists to offer then. He makes a request for these and for a supply of samples. In a another fax of the same date, he is more specific, and addresses only Elvor. The buyer, through *EasternTex*, wants to know if they can supply, from stock, a fabric called *Cortina-Peach* in black. Alternative colours might be acceptable, but they need to know what quantities can be supplied. *Cortina-Peach*, it becomes later apparent, is a dirt and moisture repellent fabric, and has been part of *Aviator*'s regular range as recently as 1990.

The response, received next day from Elvor, is disappointing. No black is available — and no substantial quantities in other colours. The remaining lengths vary between 20 and 250 metres, and most of these are of second quality. It is not possible to explain on the basis of the available data why Lenny, as a merchandiser, should depend on his superior for this information nor why, once the required information has been supplied, he should seem unaware of its implications. In his next fax to Stephen at *EasternTex* he asks:

Please advise whether you need to place order for black color.

It seems likely that Lenny intends to enquire whether *colour* (as distinct from texture and weight) is the critical factor, and that Stephen interprets the message to mean that black *is* in fact available, and that if an order is received it can be met. On 15th August, Lenny faxes again, apologising for delay, and promising further information, based on results of an enquiry made by *Aviator* of the manufacturer of the fabric in question. That day, he also sends a fax to the head office with the information that material of second-rate quality *would* be acceptable to the buyer, since it is, in the first place, needed only for the making up of samples. About 50 metres would be enough, and the buyer would settle for any dark colour — navy blue, say, or purple, if the preferred black cannot be supplied. What can she offer?

The response is not among the records, but it seems to have been negative, since four days later, on 19th August, Lenny faxes again, asking for 10m samples of any colour, even a light colour, to satisfy the client's requirement — by this time an urgent matter. This request is repeated the following day and over written with what looks like the gist of a telephoned answer to the effect that colour no. 3800 will be sent. The promise is welcome, and the following day Lenny faxes his thanks to Elvor, and asks that the material shall be sent immediately —

the most fastest way to EasternTex and advise details.

However, by 29th August, more than a week later, the prospective buyer has received nothing, and is growing impatient. So Lenny faxes a reminder to Elvor, and her answer is overwritten on his copy of the fax — the fabric was sent on 20th August, she says, and should be received during that week.

There is, however, no sign of it when Lenny faxes again, on 2nd September and a silence until 25th September, when Lenny faxes a repetition of his request. This brings an immediate response in the form of a table of ten colours of which 50m or more remain. It seems that the Hong Kong buying office and their Japanese customer accept this delayed reply, for on 29th September, Lenny is able to report to Elvor that the customer is still very interested in *Cortina-Peach*, and would like to know exactly what quantities are available in each colour. It seems that this is a serious buyer, and that progress is being made, even if uncertainly, towards a deal.

Negotiations go forward

Within a few days, Lenny reports that the buyer is ready to place an order for small quantities in each of two available colours, and he asks Elvor to make sure that they are quickly despatched, only to meet with a further setback. The fax is overwritten with what looks like the note of a telephoned response:

sorry Lenny but 3745 is outsold already.

This number, 3745, stands for grey/khaki. However, as Lenny informs Elvor on 9th October, the buyer is willing to settle for 3637 — green/khaki. On 15th October, Lenny faxes a reminder — and must be puzzled by Elvor's response: what does he mean? how many metres? and in what colour? In reply, Lenny faxes details of the order, which ignores the information offered on 25th

September, and requests 1000m in each of four colours, black, natural, royal (blue) and grey, at a cost of USD6.00 per metre. On the same day, but in a separate fax, Lenny asks Elvor if there is any way at all in which this order can be met and explains the anxiety and persistence of the potential buyer — who is, it now appears, committed to using this fabric in completing an order not only for the Japanese client, but also for another, a Swedish buyer. A copy of a Purchase Order, sent from *EasternTex* to *Aviator*, and confirming the details, is appended, dated 15th October. It brings a predictably negative response from Elvor.

> **There is absolutely no solution to this. we have nothing at all left and no quality similar to Cortina.**

She suggests, not at all hopefully, that the buyer might be willing to consider the use of an alternative fabric. That same day, Lenny receives another fax from her, this time expressed with more asperity —

> **we do not have Cortina greige fabric. I thought this would have been clear already after all the fax correspondence concerning how little we have left of this fabric. Cortina and Cortina-Peach have not been in our collections after last Autumn, which you can see from the material you have been receiving from us.**

It is hard not to sympathise with Elvor's evident irritation. Lenny seems not to take in or act in accordance with information available to him. It is as if, lacking experience of the business, he is without the contextual information that would give meaning to her assertions.

Lenny is not, however, at the end of his resources yet. The next day, October 18th, he faxes a colleague in another office of the company, ostensibly on an unrelated matter, and asks if *he* has any solution to the problem? — only to get a decisive *no*. There is no fabric left. The quantity required is too small to warrant weaving additional stock, and even if that were practicable, they have no supplies of the yarn needed for the warp. There is no alternative for Lenny but to fax Stephen in the *EasternTex* office and admit, belatedly, that no fabric is available in the required colour; that his request to the Head Office asking for an exceptional special delivery has been unsuccessful, and to conclude with a formula likely to irritate the recipient by minimising the disappointment of a reasonable expectation:

Sorry for any inconvenience caused.

On the same day, Lenny asks Elvor to return the contract to him, and the colour swatches, and tells her he has explained the reasons why it is not possible to accept the proposed contract. He is, however, still very reluctant to let the deal go.

An alternative proposal

Two days later, on 23rd October, he faxes Elvor at the head office again to say that he wants to offer the disappointed customer an alternative fabric, *Microspirit Peach*. (The similar name may suggest that the texture, at least, may not be too dissimilar from *Cortina Peach*) He asks her, as a matter of urgency, to let him know how much of the fabric could be supplied, and at what price? He gets a reply next day. This fabric *is* available in the colour required. The price is quoted, this time as DM12.15. Lenny informs the buyer at once, and is able, on 28th October, to go back to Elvor to enquire as to the best available delivery time, and whether a lower price could be offered. Next day, he faxes again to confirm that the buyer will accept *Microspirit Peach*, but that the price quoted is perceived as too high. Can a discount be offered, in the interests of goodwill in the longer term? Also, can he have an immediate answer? In her reply, dated 29th October, Elvor agrees to immediate delivery of the material — but only on condition that the buyer accepts two colours currently in production, instead of the Royal and the Grey that they specify. Where Lenny had expected a concession, out of consideration for the disappointment and delay experienced by the buyer, Elvor instead imposes further conditions. Lenny is asked to check that they will agree and to respond immediately.

Cancellation

The conditions that the buyer should compromise over the preferred colour proves to be the last straw. That day, Lenny receives a fax couched very differently from the hitherto informal and laconic style. It starts ominously:

We would like to lodge a strong complaint against your company

and continues by recounting, in detail, the story from the disappointed buyer's standpoint. They have, they say, put effort and resources into the promotion of *Aviator* products, and have succeeded — only then to be disappointed at the refusal of an order, and to find that the mill was unable to supply the fabric in the required colour. This deal was the first purchase of goods supplied to a Japanese customer, and as a direct consequence of their — *EasternTex's* — recommendation. Nor did the loss of credibility suffered in consequence stop there. The recommended alternative, *Microspirit Peach*, was accepted by the Japanese buyer. *Aviator* had said that since it was offered as a substitute, it would be offered at a reduced price (someone — presumably Lenny — has overwritten at this point *"we never mention this"*), and *then* the buyer was asked to accept not a lower, but an increased, price — and that in addition to standard colours not matching his requirements.

The final sentence seems, however, to indicate that despite all the indignation expressed, the door is not at that point, finally closed on the deal —

> **We look forward to receiving your prompt reply regarding an earlier delivery, a reduction in price, and your consent to dye the colors of the customers choice.**

A week later, Stephen, at *EasternTex*, following telephone calls to them both, sends a more temperately expressed fax to Elvor, and copies it to Lenny. There will be no deal. The Japanese client has cancelled the order, he thanks the company for accepting the cancellation, and offers an apology to a colleague of Elvor, who had, though unsuccessfully, gone out of his way to assist them in meeting the order.

Lenny confirms acceptance of the cancellation in a fax to Stephen. He is more blunt in his fax to Elvor — his view is that *EasternTex*, as the buyer for the Japanese client, should share with *Aviator* the costs of failure, and should at least bear the courier charges if *Aviator* accepts the production loss. Lenny, it is evident, recognises the reality of the transaction costs of a deal, and knows that these have to be met, independently of whether the deal in question is brought to a satisfactory and profitable conclusion or not.

Nobody reading the set of faxes from which the script is reconstructed could fail to be impressed by Lenny's persistence in furthering the interests of the company, or by the anxiety on the part of Stephen that the deal for which they have responsibility should succeed. Why then the failure, expensive financially, and costly in terms of the time expended and the goodwill lost?

Causes of failure

There is no reason to think that the use by Lenny and by Elvor of a language native to neither of them played any significant part in the collapse of this transaction, except on a single occasion, described above, where Lenny seems not to realise that his statement will bear an interpretation quite different from that which he intends. Both correspondents write fluently and seem not to experience difficulty with linguistic comprehension. With hindsight, it seems that though the deal could not have been brought to a conclusion in which both parties were entirely satisfied, much wasted time and some ill-feeling could have been avoided. A concession by Elvor in terms of a discounted price on the substitute fabric would probably have been accepted by the buyer. The financial loss would have been no greater than that of the subsequent cancellation, and the loss of standing and goodwill very much less.

The Japanese buyers seem not to have known, and should have been told, through their agents, that in a business where goods are regularly supplied to the customers, stocks of fabric are not routinely maintained from one season to the next. Lenny should have had access to information about exactly what could be supplied. He regarded the information he received to be late and inconsistent: it may well have been that Elvor over-estimated the extent of his knowledge of the business. He, Lenny, seems to have compounded his mistakes by taking the initiative in offering a substitute that was part of the supplier's current range. In the absence of a clear statement to the contrary, it was natural enough for a buyer to suppose that a material offered as a substitute for that initially ordered, and lighter in weight, would be less, rather than more expensive. Lenny's indignation at the charge that he said it would be cheaper may be natural, but from the buyer's standpoint, is unjustified. Lenny's position was additionally compromised by Elvor's insistence that the buyer must accept a choice from the current range of colours, and that there could be no question of dyeing some part of it to meet the special requirement of the order. That condition, coming as it did when he had given way on the fabric and been disappointed at the price, was predictably experienced by the buyer as an affront. A sequence of mistakes, some, but not all of them, attributable to the inexperience of a merchandiser undertaking responsibilities beyond his competence, contributed to failure. The only remarkable feature of these mistakes is that they are exceptional and infrequent.

4.5 Success

The companies and the products

Two companies were involved in the faxed correspondence on which this study is based, *Irish Girl* in Macau, and a Southern England-based buyer, which imports for distribution to retailers countrywide the women's and children's underwear and night-wear in which *Irish Girl* specialises. The English company uses its own brand name for the imported garments, and makes it a condition of trading that there shall be no indication of the country of origin in the labelling. The Macau supplier obtains the materials, largely delicate fabrics from Japan, and arranges for the actual manufacturing to be done in China. Even by the standards of South East Asia, this is a high-risk and high-profit business. The faxed correspondence is evidence of the extent to which supplier and buyer collaboratively develop strategies to reduce the risk, and maximise the profit. The result is markedly successful enterprise, as was apparent on our second visit to the Macau company eight months after the first. On arrival, we found that the former premises were in use as warehouse space — the company's office had been obliged to move, to make room for the rapid rate of expansion, and to accommodate an increasingly up-market image.

A single senior employee, Terry, is responsible for the faxed communication on which the business depends. He is the only person in the company who would claim a high level of fluency in English, and his working day is almost exclusively occupied with faxed communication. No concessions to the fact that he is operating in a second language are made by the English buyers. They give no indication of being aware of the possibility of less than immediate and complete comprehension, and on the rare occasions when they do not fully understand him, they brusquely demand an explanation. Misunderstandings arise from time to time, but from non-linguistic grounds.

The Macau and Southern England offices operate differently. The work that falls on a single merchandiser in Macau is, in the English office, distributed among a number of employees, so there is less pressure on any one of them. In part, no doubt, as a result, our file includes records of their regular meetings at which progress on all the deals currently going forward are subject to critical review and discussion. The records are headed *Agenda*, but comprise reports of information submitted and decisions made — they are what is usually understood as *Minutes*. The Macau office, in contrast, works under a constant pressure of time that virtually excludes reflective or strategic deliberation.

Deals going forward in spring 1991

The material selected for this case study comprises all the faxes exchanged between supplier and buyer over an arbitrarily chosen period of three months, January to March 1991. Five deals were then at different stages of progress between the two companies. Except in formal documents like *Purchase Orders*, where the code number is set out with the description of the item, the correspondence refers to the items only by the numbers used to differentiate them. All the deals relate to women's brassieres in various fabrics and designs. The production of these items, mainly because of the problems of sewing and dyeing associated with soft and fine fabrics, including elastic, is complicated and costly. The code numbers and descriptions are tabled below.

Item No.	***Description***
4216	white, full cup
4218	white, embroidered, under-wired
4219	white cotton, soft cup
4220	white cotton, under-wired
91/28-4	nylon fabric and nylon lace

Of these items, the first four are repeat orders. The last is new in the period under scrutiny. On a recent visit to Hong Kong, a senior representative of the

English company saw a sample of 91/28-4, and identified it as an attractive, and potentially highly saleable product in their retail markets. It is made of nylon fabric and nylon lace, dyed to match, in three styles and four colours. Because of its novelty, it occupies more of the correspondence than the others.

The purchasing order for the first four is dated 19th February, and the March faxes negotiate the shipping and delivery dates. By the end of March, the deal on 91/28-4 has reached only the much earlier stage of approval of samples. Virtually every fax relates to every deal, and there is some possibility of confusion between them, even where, as is certainly the case, the correspondents are thoroughly familiar with the business. One purpose of choosing this case for study is to indicate the volume and the value of trading routinely handled.

In the interests of conciseness, the content of the faxes has been summarised and set out in the form of tables below, so that the development of each deal, whether smooth or dogged with setbacks, can be readily traced without the need for extensive citation. Only the buyer assigns a number to each fax sent. *Irish Girl* employs no such system, but is careful about the inclusion of dates. In referring to future dates, for example when negotiating delivery dates, both companies number the weeks from the start of the calendar year in January.

The two companies adopt the same organisation of the text to be communicated. Each deal currently in progress is usually — but not consistently — the subject of a separate, numbered section, having the code number of the item as an underlined heading. The same order is observed in the response, and is undisturbed through a sequence of faxes. Confusion is thus less likely and it is not difficult for participants to check, or for observers to trace, the fortunes of a particular transaction. There are emerging practices, not yet deliberate, nor consistent.

Three months' trading: An overview

The summary and shortened paraphrase set out in the tables below demonstrates how extensive the text generated by a few months of trading is. Of the five deals, four are already known to be successful in the market. Quantities are large, based, it can be assumed, on the experience of earlier sales, and it is noticeable how little negotiation is required over price — the English company is willing to pay the prices asked in Macau, and it is fair to infer that the prices are low enough to allow for substantial profits. Expressed concerns are over available quantities and despatch dates. Export quotas trouble neither supplier or buyer. Where *Irish Girl* reach the limits of their permitted quota, they employ the alternative Denmark route. Even when the strong yen and the consequent increased cost of imports from Japan are passed on to the buyers, they raise no objection. These deals proceed as rapidly as the import of materials, the processes of manufacture, and the availability of shipping, will allow.

The new item (91/28-4) is less straightforward. The buyers make no comment on hearing what might be presumably disappointing news — that the item is already on sale in the United Kingdom. They readily accept an experienced merchandiser's solution — the offer of a similar, but distinct design, which will be unique to their range. The problems which arise do so from the conviction that an article so attractive has the potential for very large sales. They want it in April — in time for its inclusion in their retailers' spring ranges. They would settle for white only, if that concession would secure an early delivery date. In response, it is explained that the dyeing required for a perfect match between the fabrics used can be done only in the country of origin. It is beyond the capacity of a Macau-based company to bring forward the production process to suit the seasonal demands of the U.K. market — just as in two of the other cases (nos. 4219 and 4220), the supplier cannot hasten the delivery of those items which are made of soft cotton, the sewing of which must necessarily be slow.

Anxiety is evident in the correspondence, and stems from more than one cause. One is the rapid rate of response expected. For the buyer, the principal source of unease is delay in the delivery of goods with potential consequent loss of seasonal sales, and with it, of the goodwill of retailers. Lead times are always too long. Some styles sell better in some sizes than in others, and it seems not possible for the buyer to predict the variation at the time of making the purchase order. Hence the demand, a difficult one for the supplier, of supplementary orders in certain sizes only. For the supplier, anxiety arises not only from the unremitting pressure for rapid delivery of orders, irrespective of whether or not the causes of delay are within his control, but also from the difficulty experienced in getting paid for goods already sent. Large debts are allowed to accumulate. This is serious for any business, but threatens real trouble for the textile trade in South East Asia, where stock is not kept, and materials for each transaction are purchased as they are required, always in advance of payment. They depend on banks to finance the required expenditure and on prompt payment to repay the loan. Within the three months included in this case study, the supplier makes four complaints of delays in payment; has the satisfaction of an apology (on 5th February) and a promise of immediate payment (on 21st February). In the same period the buyer too has complaints to make, and their complaints are always of shortcomings in communication, of delays in answers to faxes, of failure to reply directly to the points made in a fax, of delays in sending samples requested, and of neglect of reminders. The tables that conclude the chapter indicate how complex and demanding are the tasks that merchandisers regularly undertake.

Strategies for resolving problems

The difficulties admit of no easy solution, but they are the problems of success. The buyers *seem* to be entirely incurious about the difficulties Terry obviously has in shortening lead times and securing prompt delivery of orders. However, to say this may well be unjust to the English company. In May 1991 — soon after the end of this section of arbitrarily selected correspondence, a senior member of the English company made a visit to Macau, with the intention (as is clear from his thanks for hospitality) of obtaining insight into the operation of Macau-based companies. Soon after the visit, in June 1991, the company set up a buying office based in Hong Kong and staffed by Cantonese speaking employees. Faxed correspondence with Macau continued, in English. Though the intention must have been to speed and smooth the interaction between supplier and buyer, there is little evidence in the faxed correspondence that this was the effect. Difficulties recorded in the exchange became, on the contrary, more numerous, and the tone more uneasy than in that selected for this study. Trade continued, however, to go well for both parties. The English company has a source of products available at prices that suit their market, are free to use their own brand name, and avoid, at their own insistence, a label that informs the eventual customer of the actual place of origin. The *Irish Girl* merchandiser has a buyer for larger quantities than he can easily supply, on terms he finds acceptable, and a buyer willing to pay, without cavil, the prices he asks. Each has the strongest possible incentive to continue such a satisfactory state of affairs. Charges of dilatoriness are absorbed without comment and delayed

Table 9.
Deal 4216
(full cup bra, white, price HKD17.00/piece for sizes B,C, HKD18.20/piece size D)

Date	*Fax No*	*Sender*	*Message*
29th Jan.	7730/91	English buyer	Queries the shipment of 10,000 pieces: whenis the best delivery date on an order placed that week?
1st Feb.		*Irish Girl*	Reply: order for 10,000 pieces could be delivered in week 27. Prices quoted.
No date	7751/9	Buyer	Disappointment at suggested delivery date: Anxiety expressed for quantities in popular sizes: suggests 5,000 pieces as soon as possible, remainder on 1st July. Prices approved.
2nd Feb.		*Irish Girl*	Material not sufficient for more than 5,000 pieces — best offer 5,000 pieces by week 21 via Denmark — and balance in week 27.
5th Feb.		*Irish Girl*	Request for confirmation of order by mid-Feb. as condition of promised delivery.
5th Feb.	7764/91	Buyer	Popular sizes of this item do not coincide with the quantities ordered. Could increase the total order to 15,000 pieces if 2,500 in the popular sizes could be despatched immediately — the balance in weeks 21 and 37.
6th Feb.		*Irish Girl*	Request to expect 2,500 pieces in week 17, via Denmark, the balance in week 25.
9th Feb.		*Irish Girl*	Complaint of delayed payment on this and other items.
11th Feb.		*Irish Girl*	Request for answer to query before the holiday — without confirmation there may be further delay.
19th Feb.		Buyer	Order attached with details of packing, shipment, mode of payment.

payments are made, before a critical stage is reached. Functional communicative practice emerges from the trading processes which it sustains.

Table 10
Deal 4218
(embroidered and under-wired bra, in white, price HKD 16.00 for sizes B and C, HKD17.10 for D)

Date	***Fax No.***	***Sender***	***Message***
29th Jan.	7730/91	English buyer	Query about earliest delivery date on an order placed this week?
1st Feb.		*Irish Girl*	Delivery in week 27: prices offered: an 1st July?
2nd Feb.		*Irish Girl*	Answer is 5,000 pieces by week 21, remainder by week 27.
5th Feb.		*Irish Girl*	Request to confirm acceptability of dates before Chinese New Year holiday
5th Feb.	7764/91	Buyer	Same problem as with 4216 — some sizes are more popular than was predicted. 2,500 pieces are needed as soon as possible, or in week 21, remainder in week 27.
6th Feb.		*Irish Girl*	Best offer is 2500 in week 17, via Denmark, balance in week 25.
9th Feb.		*Irish Girl*	Request to answer query about payment in respect of this item.
11th Feb.		*Irish Girl*	Request for confirmation of the order before the Chinese New Year holiday.
19th Feb.	7803/91	Buyer	Order nos. 5250, 5251, 5252 include this with other items.

Table 11
Deal 4219
(Cotton soft-cup bra, in white, price HKD14.10/piece)

Date	***Fax No.***	***Sender***	***Message***
29th Jan.	7730/91	English buyer	Request for confirmation of delivery time.
1st Feb.		*Irish Girl*	Undertake to inform regarding name of vessel to be used on the following Monday.
5th Feb.	7764/91	Buyer	Advice of intention to place an order, with request for earliest ETD, and shipment detail.
6th Feb.		*Irish Girl*	Best ETD[a] is week 27 for orders placed before the Chinese New Year holiday. Explanation of increased price – it is the effect of the strong yen on the price of cotton imported from Japan. Delay is the effect of the softness of the fabric – the sewing process is slow.
9th Feb.		*Irish Girl*	This item is among those products supplied for which payment is overdue.
19th Feb.	7803/91	Buyer	This item included in purchase orders 5250, 5251, 5252.
13th March	7855/91	Buyer	Query about delivery time on 4219 and 4220.
25th March	7920/91	Buyer	Request for details of shipment. This consignment should have been shipped in Feb. No information, and no response to last fax, have been received.
27th March	7955/91	Buyer	Further query – was this item shipped on the vessel *Laust Maerak*?

[a]ETD — estimated time of delivery.

Table 12
Deal 4220
(Cotton under-wired bra, in white, price HKD15.80/piece)

Date	***Fax No.***		
29th Jan.	7730/91	Buyer	Request for confirmation of delivery time.
1st Feb.		*Irish Girl*	Promise to inform of name of vessel by the following Monday.
no date	7751/91	Buyer	Repeat request for name of vessel, ETD, quantity, and route.
5th Feb.	7764/91	Buyer	Informs of intention to place an order: Requests ETD
6th Feb.		*Irish Girl*	ETD is week 27: increased price is the effect of strong *yen* on the cost of cotton; original ETD was 25th Jan. — but order unlikely to be completed before CNY. Soft fabric delays sewing. Half the order can be expected in week 11.
9th Feb.		*Irish Girl*	This item is among those for which payment is overdue.
19th Feb.	7803/91	Buyer	Item included in purchasing orders 5250, 5251, 5252.
13th March	7885/91	Buyer	Request for information about delivery — items should have left Macau
25th March	7920/91	Buyer	Another request for information about shipment.
27th March	7955/91	Buyer	Request to confirm if the shipment is on the *Laust Maerak*

Table 13
Deal 28-4/91
(a nylon and lace bra in three styles and four colours)

Date	***Fax No.***	***Sender***	***Message***
30th Jan.	7735/91	Buyer	Request to place an order for item seen in Hong Kong — quantities required by size and colour, Enquiries about EDT — asks for urgent response.
1st Feb.	746/91	Buyer	Repeated request for immediate reply
1st Feb.		*Irish Girl*	The item is already supplied to the UK market. Could produce a similar design. Best delivery is week 27. Must have a minimum order of 6,000 pieces — this is the minimum required for the dyeing process.
no date	7751/91	Buyer	Response must await Mr. Power's return
4th Feb.	7758/91	Buyer	1 - Slight design difference acceptable; 2 - Samples wanted by return 3 - as is an April delivery date 4 - Coloured as well as white samples are requested
5th Feb.		*Irish Girl*	A problem — no matching fabric and lace in pink, peach, or aqua. Dyeing must be done in Japan, so week 27 is the best delivery date available.
6th Feb.	7769/91	Buyer	Repeats requests for delivery date and samples in colour.
8th Feb.	7779/91	Buyer	Query about date for samples. If they settle for white only, can an April delivery date be met? Request for urgent reply.
9th Feb.		*Irish Girl*	Samples are being made and will be sent in week 9 — and will include coloured items. Sorry cannot meet April delivery date.

Table 13
Continued

Date	*Fax No.*	*Sender*	*Message*
1st March	7826/91	Buyer	Request to send 12pcs in each of 3 colours. Large orders are expected.
4th March	7835/91	Buyer	Request for an urgent reply.
5th March		*Irish Girl*	Failed to receive fax dated 1st March: samples were sent the day before, in white and pink: approval needed for the other colours.
5th March		*Irish Girl*	Colour swatch enclosed.
14th March	7890/91	Buyer	No samples received yet. What has been sent? Request for urgent reply to fax of 13th March.
21st March	7906/91	Buyer	Just received sample. Acceptable — likely to be a winner in fact — but there were in the original sample three different styles. Can these be made using the new lace?

Chapter 5

Towards a Description of *Trade English*

Business English has been recently and authoritatively described in these terms:

> "The most important characteristic of exchanges in the context of business meetings, telephone calls and discussions, is a sense of purpose. Language is used to achieve an end, and its successful use is seen in terms of a successful outcome to the business transaction or event. ... Much of the language needed by business people will be transactional: getting what you want and persuading others to agree with the course of action you propose. The language will frequently be objective rather than subjective and personal." (Ellis and Johnson, 1994: 7–8)

This is an intentionally very general description and is in those general terms applicable to faxed correspondence. It is possible at this stage to be more specific. The language used to implement a trade deal shares the potential of the deal itself, that of making both parties better off. Just as buyer and supplier each have a strong incentive to succeed in an essentially collaborative undertaking, senders and receivers of faxed messages have a powerful motive to communicate and to interpret them efficiently. The language they use is a resource in the sense that it enables the additional value embodied in the exchange to materialise.

As a resource, the efficient use of language is an issue. The data we have collected from trade transactions demonstrates the emergence of a variety of English that might be called *TradeSpeak*, which users believe to be more economical, accessible and effective than the Standard English (written) they studied in school. It is not, of course, suggested that their use of it is always a matter of deliberate choice, or that their operational knowledge of it is articulate and accessible to their scrutiny. Therefore, the excerpts that follow demonstrate not only an orderliness in *TradeSpeak*, but also its unsettled and unstable, even experimental character. The intention is to indicate the purposeful and economical character of *TradeSpeak*, and the limitations and the risks associated with its use.

References were made at a number of points in earlier chapters to examples from texts. These were intended as illustrations and kept deliberately brief so as not to interrupt the flow of the argument. There are stronger reasons than additional illustration for the inclusion, in this chapter, of more extended and more fully contextualised citations.

From large overall considerations in the first chapter, we moved to consideration of the industrial organisation of the trade in garment and textiles located in the Pearl River Delta, and from there, to an account of a text-based investigation into the recent trade procedures of a sample of companies in Chapter 3. Chapter 4 demonstrates that the generation of texts in the process of the continuous communication that accompanies a trade transaction is so indispensable and so dense, that deals and parts of deals can be reconstructed from the texts they generate.

Chapter 5 continues this concept of a progressive narrowing of focus. It offers selected examples of text, with paraphrase, focusing on what is at once indispensable to, and generated by, trade deals. Transcriptions follow the original as closely as is consistent with the anonymity of sources. Dates, and names by which merchandisers prefer to be known (either English names or the initials of Chinese given names) are retained. Knowledge of context is shown to disambiguate text, though not always, sufficiently. Our intention is to offer the reader a lens for scrutiny of the detailed texture of trade deals, and a sense of how merchandisers actually operate, as they receive and comprehend incoming faxes, frame and despatch replies. The contention is that the ability to communicate effectively is an important factor in the explanation of trading success on the micro, i.e. the business level, and consequently on the aggregated, macro-level too.

5.1 Abbreviation and Ellipsis

Text

This first illustrative faxed exchange was part of the correspondence in a trade deal between a Macau-based export company and an international counterpart based in New York. The deal was at an early and crucial stage, when samples have to be provided by the supplier, and details agreed with the buyer, prior to releasing the (already confirmed) order for production. The garments in question were jackets.

The company in Macau is *Songster*, trading with buyers in New York. At the Macau end, there are two senior and experienced merchandisers, Priscilla and S.Y. They correspond with two employees in New York, Dick and Kerry. Sometimes a third, Lisa, also in New York, is involved. The product is regularly referred to in correspondence by code number. Those referred to in this exchange are:

- **S 51680-67277**, a sample of which is being made in black and
- **S 51871-75186**, where medium size samples are being made up in two colours — fiery red and batik blue.

There are references to two more deals: *Songster* has still to receive comments on these. The first item, the black jacket, is the one presenting some difficulty at this point; several changes are required, and Priscilla has, within the last week, received a faxed set of labelled drawings indicating these.

The text of the exchange, starting on 27th July, follows.

Attn. Dick /Kerry
AA RE CRRTN FR STY S51680-67277X
91/7/27

1 RE PT 1 X DO U MEAN THE HEIGHT OF LBL PATCH X IF SO X IT SEEMS TOO LONG FR THIS SZ N THE SZ OF SMPL IS SAME AS PAST X BESIDES X V HV BKD FAB WHICH WAS BASED ON THIS SZ TO FIGURE SO THE BULK FAB WL NOT ENOUGH FR PRODTN X PLS KINDLY U/STAND N CFM KEEP 3-1/2 " AS OUR SMPL X

2 RE PT 3 TO 5 X NTD N WL CRRT DURING PRODTN X

3 RE PT 6X AS PER YR ORD DTLS THAT THE HEIGHT OF BACK YOKE IS 2-1/2"
NOT 3-1/2 X SO V HV BKD FAB FR PRODTN N FAB MILL CAN'T ACCEPT ANY
CHANGE X O/W X WL AFFECT THE FAB DEL X PLS U/STAND N CONSIDER
TO KEEP HEIGHT AS ORIGINAL X PLS ADV BACK X

BB RE STY S51871-75186 ,C11976 N KRUJ21979 X HV BN SENT SMPL TO U X Sty S51871-75186,C11976 AND KRUJ21979 PLS ADV YR CRRTN SOONEST X

TKS. RGDS

Within two days, there is a three-page faxed response from New York, including another drawing of one of the details of construction — the back facing of the jacket:

7/29/91

1) ADV ADD. QNTY YOU CAN MAKE IN STYLE C11976 FOR NOV ND DEC

2) RE AA S51680-67277:
(A) YR PT 1 SEE ATTACHED
B) YR PT 2 NTD (C) YR PT 3 CNFM TO KEEP YOKE AT 2 1/2 AS ORIGINAL SKETCH

3) RE PT BB (A) S51871-75186 WAS SENT ON 7/24 RESENDING SEE ENCLOSED

(B) C11976 WL ADV TMRW

C) KRU J21979 -PLS ADV AWB AND SHIP DATE AS WE HV NOT RCVD
KRU J21979

RGDS

The second and third pages are treated as enclosures. They bear the same date and identify the garment by code number, colour, and sample size. The second page includes a labelled drawing of the garment, opened to show the collar and the back facing, and has this addition:

THE BACK FACING REPLACING THE LINING IS TOO SHORT IT MEASURES 3 1/2 LONG .IT SHOULD MEASURE 4 1/2 " LONG (I'M NOT TALKING ABOUT LBL PATCH)

The original fax has a handwritten addition without evidence of authorship.

CFM U WL CRRCT

The third page relates to number S 51871-75186, that is to the sample jackets to be made up in fiery red and batik blue. The comments are these:

1 PLEASE USE NON WOVEN INTERFACING UNDER LIGHT COLORS TO AVOID DARK COLORS SHOWING THROUGH

2) PLEASE MATCH COLORS ACCORDING TO YOUR COLOR CARD

3) BACK LENGTH FOR JKTS MEASURE 19 1/2 SHOULD MEASURE 20" (FIERY RED & BATIK BLUE COLORWAYS)

Interpretation

The language is a means to an end: both parties are concerned to get what they want. It has the characteristics of faxed transmission already identified. Uppercase letters are used throughout. Clause and sentence boundaries are marked by X — a simplification which means that questions cannot be unmistakably distinguished from statements and is not a feature common across companies. Abbreviation and ellipsis are used ostensibly, at least, in the interests of economy of time. Some meanings, but not all, become transparent if these features are removed, as the following partial paraphrase demonstrates. However, their removal does not produce Standard English (written):

AA Regarding correction for Style Number S51680-67277.

1 Regarding Point 1. Do you mean the height of the label patch? If so it seems too long for this size and the size of sample is same as past. Besides we have booked fabric which was based on this size to figure so the bulk fabric will not be enough for production. Please kindly understand and confirm keep 3-1/2 as our sample.

2 Regarding point 3 to 5, noted and will correct during production

3 Regarding point 6 — as per your order details that the height of back yoke is 2-1/2 not 3-1/2 — so we have booked fabric for production and fabric mill can't accept any change without will affect the fabric delivery. Please understand and consider to keep height as original. Please advise back.

Regarding Style S 51871-75186, C 11976 and KRU J 21979 have been sent sample to you. Please advise your correction soonest. Thanks.

The rules, operated in respect of word abbreviation, can be easily inferred and articulated as follows:

- omit the central vowel from common words of a single syllable
- omit the second syllable of common words of two syllables
- adopt abbreviated forms based on the sounds of letters for common function words; write in full any other words

There follows an attempt at a full paraphrase, a longhand version using Standard English (written). The additions are required (as to any elliptical text) and these are italicised so as to be at once apparent:

AA Regarding correction for Style Number S51680-67277.

1 Regarding Point 1. Do you mean *to indicate by the changed figure in your previous fax a change in* the height of the label patch? If *that is the change you require the measurement* seems too long for this size and the size of sample is same *in terms of its measurements as that which was found satisfactory in* the past. Besides we have booked fabric *in a quantity* which was based on this size (to figure) so the fabric *already ordered in anticipation* of bulk order will not be enough for production. Please kindly understand *our embarrassing situation in this respect* and confirm *that we can* keep *the original size* 3-1/2 as our sample.

2 Regarding point 3 to 5, *these have been* noted and will *be* correct*ed* during production.

3 Regarding point 6 — as per your order details. It *is the case that* that the height of *the* back yoke is 2-1/2 not 3-1/2 — so we have

booked fabric for production and *our* fabric mill can't accept any change without that change affecting the time of the fabric delivery. Please understand *how they and we are placed* and consider *keeping the* height as *in the* original. Please advise us *of your decision.*

Regarding Style S51871-75186, C11976 and KRU J 21979, *all these required samples have* been sent to you. Please advise us *of your requirements for correction* soonest. Thanks.

Analysis

The differences between Standard English (written) and the paraphrased text are not random. Rules apply which can be articulated:

- Omit articles,
- Omit demonstrative adjective e.g. this, these,
- Omit auxiliary verbs, verb endings,
- Omit any items that the reader can supply from his/her knowledge of this deal,
- In brief, treat as redundant any items the reader can supply from his/her knowledge of the regular sequence of events in deals.

There is of course nothing definitive about the resulting paraphrase, and at one (bracketed) point we have indicated that we fail to understand what is meant. Nor is it suggested that this could possibly be a suitable model for use in the companies. Its purpose is simply to demonstrate how, apart from the ways detailed above, this variety that might be called *TradeSpeak* differs from the standard. What has been inserted, in addition to missing function words, is many cohesive devices, references to circumstances that one party to the correspondence assumes are so entirely present to the mind of the other, as to be predictable.

The response, two days later, plainly demonstrates that this assumption is *not* always borne out. The intended meanings are *not* always apparent. All the anxiety about the size of the label patch, and the effects of meeting the request for a larger one, rested on a misunderstanding, corrected in the response by single laconic sentence —

"I'm not talking about lbl patch"

The overwritten note **cfm u wl crrct**, if it can be paraphrased thus:

Please confirm that you will make the correction required

asks for written assurance that the substance has been correctly understood, and that appropriate action will follow. Such requests are a common and necessary strategy. This is not the end of the matter. An increased size in the back facing is likely to require an increased quantity of lining material for bulk production. We can offer no evidence of the outcome.

5.2 Varieties within *Tradespeak*

The following example is an exchange between a Macau supplier whose employees are users of English as a second language, and a North American buyer who is (almost certainly) a native speaker of English. This is the sort of correspondence that merchandisers in Hong Kong and Macau regard as particularly demanding. They are well aware of their disadvantage in terms of ease and fluency in the use of English, and of the possibility that errors may incur ridicule or criticism.

The evidence of the data is that such a reaction is unusual, but certainly not unknown. This example is representative of the contrast in the way native and non-native speakers employ English in business correspondence, and of the generally satisfactory levels of understanding that they nonetheless achieve. It illustrates, in addition, the difference between what is earlier described as *TradeSpeak* and the choice of an informal mode of written English that includes some common abbreviations and some technical terms.

Text

This text is part of an exchange between a New Jersey buyer, and a Macau merchandiser. The buyer writes the following, dated 1st March. The original text is handwritten, rapidly jotted, not easily legible.

Re ur fax 4-1
Re 57-OK

Re 892 -will advise L/C within this week-delayed due to Easter holidays
E 90/32-6
OK to use swimwear fabric on brief & bodysuit also send me sample for bra also to see if that's ok -
However -we prefer the shiny fabric -there's no shiny satinet available with two-way stretch ?
Anyway -please make sure smpls are not marked smpl on the garment only on the label.Rgds -Gary

The reply, typed and set out with underlined headings for each topic, is dated 5th March — a long enough delay to require an apology and explanation.

DEAR GARY
JUST CAME BACK FROM EUROPE ON 28/4/91

Re Art 90/32-6 N SOFT CUP 91/69
WILL HV THE SPL REMADE,THE REASON IS HAT I HV MISUNDERSTAND YR FAX ON 1-4-91 N THOUGHT THAT U ACCEPT THE WHOLE SET TO BE MADE IN SWIMWEAR FABRIC, ANYWAY, LACE N FABRIC WILL ARRIVE NEXT WEEK N WILL DO THE SPL IMMED

RE NEW COLLECTION
I HV PROMISED TO SEND U ONE MORE SET OF NEW SPL END/APR, THEY ARE JUST READY N WILL BE SENT MONDAY FOR YR ATTENTION

WHAT PARTICULARY DO U NEED PL TELL ME SO THAT I CAN CHOOSE SOME MORE

RE ART 90/32-6 COORDINATES
PL NOTE THAT THIS STYLES BEST DEL IS OCT 91 AS THE FABRIC TAKE LONG TIME TO PURCHASE NOW FROM JAPAN .IT IS NOW THE PEAK SEASON FOR KNITTING FTY EVEN V PLACE THE ORDER TOMORROW BEST DEL WILL BE END/AUG ONWARDS PL NOTE

RESHIPMENT FOR JUNE ART 368 892, 57-8-9
PL INFORM WHEN U WIL OPEN L/C FOR THESE ORDERS

BEST REGARDS - TERRY.

Interpretation

Meanings of these texts are heavily context-dependent, for the Macau supplier and the New Jersey buyer alike. The buyer signals satisfaction with two current deals, referred to by code number. Only the deal coded E90/32-6 is problematic. Samples have already been made up by the buyer: the supplier has received them and must give an immediate indication of his response. Two items of a co-ordinating set of women's underwear can be approved: he would like to see a third: He likes fabric with a glossy surface, and enquires whether such a finish is compatible with a two-way stretch (characteristic of fabric used for swim-wear and suitable for some underwear). It is important that the word *sample* should appear on an attached label, not on the garment itself. The reply from the supplier refers first to the item of most concern, and returns to it after apologising for an earlier misunderstanding about the fabric, and promising to have samples remade, as soon as the fabrics required are available. There is a promise of samples from the new (spring) collection; an explanation of the delivery time on the samples of the coordinating items, and a request for information about the date for opening Letters of Credit on three other orders. It is a routine exchange, interpretable, given a knowledge of the logical sequence that trade deals follow.

Analysis

The New Jersey buyer, almost certainly a native speaker of English, and the Macau supplier, who has an unusual degree of confidence and fluency in the language, each adopt an elliptically laconic style, intended to be direct and economical of effort and time.

The two do not, however, make similar decisions about what is time-saving, and what is redundant. The English native speaker, the buyer, makes little use of abbreviations of words. His economy of effort derives from using a style so easily colloquial that it is virtually a transcript of what could be the text of a telephone call. He has thrice used '*OK*' for a general expression of satisfaction that leaves no need to say more: He omits the first person pronoun when he believes it is perfectly evident to his reader that he is writing of himself. He does not, however, omit the devices by which cohesion of an English text is secured.

He connects and relates topics, with *also*, *however*, *anyway*, so that the reader of the brief fax *knows* how one idea suggested another to him, and without the need for explanation, what is to him important and what occurred as an afterthought. This is informally written English, not *TradeSpeak*. Like any moderately practised writer using his mother tongue, the buyer can employ styles ranging from the formal at one extreme to the very informal, approaching casualness, at the other; the determining factor is not the seriousness of the subject matter, but his/her perception of the social relation between writer and reader. He treats his supplier as a colleague with whom terms of easy familiarity are natural, and employs a use of English that (in the terms used by Giles (1977) and Giles and Powesland (1975), *converges* to the usage of his correspondent without any suggestion of that *over-accommodation*, or intentional *talking down*. The buyer moves in the direction of the supplier, without imitating his usage in a way that irritates by assuming inequality. The result is a stylistic choice that signals an intention of cordial collaboration between their respective companies.

The format of the response from the supplier is visibly different from the faxed scribble he receives: it is typed, and the headings are underlined. The first impression is of a careful and well-organised response — not however entirely borne out by the way in which the content of the faxed message is organised. The supplier assumes that his use of abbreviations will be immediately understood, and not experienced as unnecessarily cryptic, by the intended recipient of the message. The paraphrase that follows attempts to replicate the actual process of reading and understanding, by inferring and inserting missing connections and missing indications of relationships, and even then, some questions remain unresolved.

> **Re Article: 90/32-6 and soft cup 91/69**
>
> **We will have the sample re-made *(one or both samples ?).*The reason *(probably for the misunderstanding you draw attention to in your fax)* is that I have misunderstood your fax on 4th January and I thought that you *were prepared to accept that* the whole set *of co-ordinated garments should* be made up in the swim-wear fabric. Anyway *matching* lace and fabric will arrive next week and we will then do the sample *either the one requested by the buyer or the whole set* immediately .**

> **Re New Collection**
>
> **I have promised to send you one more set of the new, *that is the spring, range of* samples at the end of April. They are just now ready and they will be sent on Monday for your attention.**
>
> **If you will tell me what you particularly need, I can select some more samples *to send you in addition to those you have already shown interest in.***
>
> **Re Art 90/32-6 co-ordinates**
>
> **Please note that *the best delivery date on these* styles is October 1991 as *it* now takes a long time to obtain the fabric *which is purchased from Japan*. It is now the peak season for the knitting factory, and *even if we were* to place the order tomorrow, *the* best delivery time *would still be* from the end of August and later. Please *recognise the importance / make a note* of this.**
>
> **Re Shipment for June Articles 368,892, 57-8-9**
>
> **Please inform us when you will open Letters of Credit for these orders.**

Straightforward routine matters, like that which concludes this fax, need almost no addition, but the absence from *TradeSpeak* of plural endings means that it is not always possible to know whether the writer refers to one or several items; the casual and incomplete signalling of tenses leaves the actual sequence of past events in doubt, and conditional relationships have to be a matter for guesswork. Since each item is treated as if it were separate and discrete, the effect may be, as it is here, that the fax begins with the problematic deal 90/32-6 and then, in the third item, returns to it. The buyer, in receipt of this reply, is in possession of considerably more information than he asked for, but is still uncertain whether and when to expect the missing part of the sample, and does not know whether the sort of fabric he would ideally prefer is actually obtainable. Additional correspondence is required to put these questions with unmistakable directness. There is no barrier to doing this where, as it seems to be the case with these correspondents, the difficulties of securing information as a basis for detailed decision-making are accepted and tolerated by both parties to the transaction.

5.3 Recognition and Negative Evaluation of *TradeSpeak*

The fax, quoted below in full, was sent from a Canadian company, based in Toronto, to *Songster* in Macau, and marked for the attention of one of the senior merchandisers, although it is addressed to the director of the company. References are made to several current deals, but this fax is not intended to monitor any of them. The fax is a complaint on behalf of a colleague (Felicia) of confusion and contradiction in the handling of transactions, and specifically of the language used in the conduct of business, language which is found virtually incomprehensible by Canadians and perceived by them as wilfully obscure.

Text

WHAT IS GOING ON OVER THERE?
FELICIA CALLED AGAIN TODAY AND IS HAVING ANOTHER HEART ATTACK BECAUSE THE FAX FROM S Y WONG /M.F. KONG /PRISCILLA DATED 91/12/17 DOES NOT MAKE ANY SENSE !!!

ON HER FAX # 8019 PAGE 1 DEC.05 1991 , SHE HAS STATED VERY PLAINLY THAT SHE HAS DECIDED TO PROCEED WITH GROUP #3, GROUP #7 AND STUDIO J GROUP #5 ONLY !!!

NOW SHE HAS RECEIVED YOUR FAX THAT IS TELLING HER ALL ABOUT ALL THESE OTHER GROUPS THAT ARE NOT PART OF YOUR BUSINESS WITH HER .MOREOVER YOU MAKE NO MENTION OF GROUP #7 THAT SHE DID WANT YOU TO DO
MOREOVER YOU CALL THE COLORS NAMES THAT SHE HAS NEVER HEARD OF
GROUP #5 YOU MENTION TURQUOISE .THERE IS NO SUCH THING IN GROUP FIVE .
AS YOU CAN IMAGINE SHE REALLY HAS LOST FAITH AGAIN. I DON'T KNOW HOW MANY CHANCES WE ARE GOING TO GET BUT ENOUGH IS ENOUGH ! !

PLEASE HAVE YOUR FACTORY DO THIS RIGHT .PLEASE ASK THEM NOT TO ABBREVIATE SO MANY WORDS THIS JUST MAKES IT IMPOSSIBLE FOR ANYONE IN CANADA TO UNDERSTAND. WE ARE NOT SECRET AGENTS. JUST AGENTS. PLEASE CALL FELICIA AGAIN AND TELL HER THAT WE ARE NOT CRAZY MAYBE SHE WILL STILL LET US DO THEIR PRODUCTION IF YOU CAN GET YOUR FACTORY TO UNDERSTAND WHAT SHE NEEDS
DO YOU HAVE ALL THESE MISUNDERSTANDINGS WITH THE UNITED STATESAS WELL? IF NOT, WHY?
CAN YOU CONFIRM THAT THE SHIRTS FOR L.M. ARE STILL BEING PRODUCED?
BEST REGARDS

Interpretation

There are difficulties in confirming from other sources the information given by the writer of this irritated fax. The letter she mentions and paraphrases, written on 17th December 1991, is not part of the data collection, nor is there any other correspondence with this Canada based company. The writer's own employment status is not easy to determine: though based in Canada, she evidently identifies with the Macau supplier ("I don't know how many chances we are going to get") and is in touch with Felicia, who acts for the buyer. She uses the term *group* to mean a number of items included in a single deal; elsewhere in the correspondence, and in transactions with other companies, the term *program* is used.

It seems that the order of events was as follows: Felicia, for the buyer, faxed on 5th December an intention of proceeding with a deal in groups 3, 7, and 5; effectively, she placed an order for those items. In response, the merchandiser acting for the supplier in Macau returned what she perceived as irrelevant information about groups other than these, making no reference to group 7, and leaving Felicia annoyed and puzzled, unable to determine whether the order could proceed or not. That was bad enough in itself, but there were other sources of annoyance. The colour names used in Macau were unrecognisable in Canada. Here the writer has identified a significant issue, though there is no sign that she is aware that there is, in principle, an easy solution. A colour coding system exists, in which every one of many thousands of shades is identified by number — but its use is expensive, and smaller companies avoid the expense, and in any case, have a preference for evocative, unambiguous colour names (Cencig, 1990). The third complaint relates specifically to *TradeSpeak*: the use of frequent abbreviations makes the faxes extremely difficult for Canadians, native speakers of English, to interpret. The sender of this fax writes as if entirely unaware of working practices in Macau and believed faxed communication to be issued from the factories:

> **"Please have your factory do this right."**

It is impossible to know whether this is an error of understanding or an attempt to avoid accusing her correspondent of incompetence. She wants the Macau suppliers to telephone and reassure Felicia that (and again she identifies with the supplier in Macau):

> ***"we are not crazy."***

There is a strong suggestion that serious loss of business may well be the outcome. There is also a suggestion (but no means of confirming or disconfirming it) that these difficulties have occurred before.

Analysis

This unguarded and irritable message provides evidence of a high level of linguistic sophistication. The writer is perfectly well aware that a specific variety of English is used in the faxed English that issues from Macau; that its most evident characteristic is its use of abbreviations; that this English differs from that produced by native speakers of English and that its differences may be found troublesome. When she irritably insists that senders of messages from Macau

> ***"get it right"***

this is not an empty phrase. It is a recognition that they could select a variety of written English approximating more closely to the Standard and, for that reason, more generally intelligible. In fact, in her view, they should do just that. She recognises how critically important to trade procedures the transmission of meanings is — if that transmission fails repeatedly, orders simply cease.

In addition, she recognises another characteristic of *TradeSpeak*; that despite the emphasis on directness and speed, dubiously relevant information is often included, and direct and necessary questions are left unanswered, or receive ambiguous replies. On at least one count she is plainly wrong; factories produce garments or process textiles; merchandisers are responsible for the communicative processes. She is almost certainly wrong, too, in supposing that a telephone call would mollify Felicia and persuade her of what is certainly the case — that Macau merchandisers are competent, business-like and astute. She might well interpret the pronunciation characteristic of Hong Kong and Macau users of English quite differently.

The writer's own English is that of a native speaker — it is not especially careful, but the sense is clear, and the feelings expressed are clearer. It is idiomatic, with no thought at all for the possibility that her reader, not a native speaker, may not understand the statement that Felicia has had a heart attack to mean that Felicia is seriously annoyed, and may not appreciate the humour in the declaration on behalf of the merchandisers in Toronto that:

> **"we are just agents, not secret agents."**

An attempt was made, during the second of the two series of visits, to ascertain what were the circumstances. The merchandiser in the Macau company recalled the letter, and said that *Songster* continued to trade amicably enough with this Canadian company, and attributed the anger of the writer to lack of experience.

5.4 Uses of Faxed English: Short- and Long-Term Negotiation

The role of the merchandiser may include more than its central function of negotiating deals to a successful conclusion. The following example illustrates the extent of the demand that an extended mediating role from time to time makes on the Hong Kong merchandiser.

The merchandiser, whose faxed correspondence provided this example, was employed as a specialist in fabric by the Hong Kong company *Aviator*. In the spring and summer of 1991, he was engaged in negotiating a deal in grey cotton/polyester fabric between a Taiwanese supplier and a Scandinavian buyer. This transaction failed to go smoothly through the usual sequence. At an early stage, the buyer, examining a sample of the product, found stripes in the direction of the warp in the supposedly plain fabric. This was the first of a series of difficulties in reconciling the buyer's requirements in terms of quality with the supplier's ability to meet them. An order was nonetheless confirmed, and a consignment of goods ready for despatch, when, upon inspection by the buyer, the fabric was found to be still defective. It was the Hong Kong merchandiser's duty to communicate this unwelcome news to the supplier's representative, only to receive from him expression of extreme dismay at what he perceived as a humiliating, personal failure, and to reply to the buyer's fax, saying that he would accept a reduced order.

Text

RE T/C 136X72 GREY CLOTH
AFTER A DISCUSSION WITH OUR FACTORY THEY DECIDED TO GIVE A TRIAL ON THIS CLOTH AND CONFIRMED FOLLOWINGS:
1/ PLEASE SHIP 10,000 M WITHIN THE ORIGINAL DELIVERY TME
2/ REST OF THE ORDER CAN BE CANCELLED.

DEAR JOHNNY , I KNOW YOU ARE TRYING TO DO BUSINESS IN A SAFETY WAY , BUT PLEASE UNDERSTAND THAT OUR FACTORY HAS ESTABLISHED OVER 170 YEARS IN FINLAND, THE WAY OF DOING BUSINESS IS VERY MUCH DIFFERENCE FROM USA MARKET , WE DO STRAIGHT BUSINESS .THE REASON WHY WE INFORMED YOU ABOUT THE FINISHING PROBLEM WAS WE WANTED TO DISCUSS THIS WITH YOU AND SEE HOW YOU CAN HELP TO SOLVE IT. PLEASE DONT GET MISUNDERSTND THAT WE WANT TO CLAIM YOU.

ANYWAY , PLEASE CONFIRM ABOVE POINT 1 + 2 URGENTLY AS OUR FACTORY WILL CLOSE FOR SUMMER HOLIDAY FROM TOMORROW
MY OPINION IS YOU SHOULD HAVE MORE CONFIDENCE IN OUR FACTORY , AND IS GOOD FOR YOUR BENIFITS FOR FUTURE BUSINESS PLEASE COMMENT . THANKS AND BEST REGARDS

Interpretation

The merchandiser's overriding concern at this stage, was that the supplier should not as a result withdraw from the international market altogether. Throughout the troubled negotiations, the Hong Kong merchandiser displayed a degree of patience that is the more remarkable given his awareness (made explicit in a fax sent to another buyer on 17th July) of the heavy penalties imposed on suppliers of sub-standard material. He encouraged the supplier to persist, not to withdraw and cancel the deal, and to accept a painstakingly negotiated compromise.

Analysis

There are effectively two distinct messages in these two paragraphs of text. The first paragraph of the fax cited is brief, business-like and direct: it records the current stage of the deal, and sets the agenda for the recipient.

What follows is entirely different, and differently encoded. It is in effect a letter employing a Standard English imperfectly learnt, which fails to encode some meanings. A narrow vocabulary obscures at some points what is almost certainly meant. In addition, the writer operates along the following rules:

- Forms that distinguish parts of speech from one another are optional and can be ignored.
- The use of cohesive devices is similarly optional
- Cohesive devices can be omitted from text since the recipient can be relied upon to understand connections and relationships between this and previous texts and internally within the text.

The following paraphrase, of the second part of the fax, expresses what may be understood as the meaning this writer would express, if he were in complete control of a language that could be fully understood by the recipient.

> **Dear Johnny, I know you are trying to do business in a *risk-minimising* way, but please understand that our factory *has been established* over 170 years in Finland, *and that* the way of doing business *in Europe* is very *different from the way business is done in* the USA market. We do business *to the very highest standards of quality.* The reason we informed you about the finishing problem**

> **was that we wanted to discuss this with you and see how *we can help you* solve it. Please do not *misunderstand us and suppose* that we want *to make an insurance claim* on you. Anyway, please confirm *the* above points 1 + 2 *as a matter of urgency* as our factory will close for the summer holiday from tomorrow.**
>
> **My opinion is you should have more confidence in our factory, and *that such confidence would be beneficial* for future business. Please comment.**
> **Thanks and best regards.**

It is not in any way surprising that this merchandiser's second language is no more than partially adequate to the demands he makes on it. What *is* a matter for remark is that he should interpret so generously his role as a mediator, explicitly recognising the supplier's good intentions despite his unsatisfactory performance, explaining what he sees as the difference between the European and the USA markets, insisting on the collaborative nature of the undertaking in which they are jointly engaged, and disclaiming any intention of making an insurance claim on behalf of the company. All this may certainly be seen as being in the long-term business interests of each party to the transaction, but it represents an unexpected *scope* in the interpretation of the mediating role.

The immediately noticeable character of this message is that for all the trouble experienced by the writer in finding a vocabulary and a sentence structure that will fully encode his meanings, what he has to say is entirely cohesive, whereas the immediately obvious characteristic of faxed trade communication, including the first part of this fax, is its discontinuity and its lack of cohesion. The layout on the page usually serves (not always) to emphasise discontinuity. Little attention is paid to ordering items on any clearly apparent principle. Faxed correspondence that forward trade deals comprises essentially disparate items, and these are of two sorts — records of action taken, and indications of the next action for the recipient to take — *minutes*, that is, and *agenda*. The resemblance between the written language associated with deals and the paperwork associated with meetings, and essential to their conduct of business, is not accidental. Prototypical faxes are the itemised *minutes* and the itemised *agenda* of business meetings among participants separated by distance, time zones, and cultures. The development of the technology of faxed correspondence makes it possible for information to be shared, for decisions to be reached and, once implemented, for the cycle to be repeated, irrespective of geographical distance; a degree of control of a common language enables the cultural and linguistic distance to be, if not ignored, at least accommodated.

5.5 A Prototype of International Trade Communication

This example of a prototypical exchange could be replicated many times in the data we have. It has its origin in the company *Irish Girl*, and it launches another deal in a sequence between this Macau company and a regular trading partner in Canada. It illustrates very usual conventions in that correspondents use the form of address and conclusion of a business letter. An enquiry is received from a potential buyer. This launches an exchange of faxes in which part of a normal structure is discernible: a sequence of three parts:

- identification;
- unsolicited information;
- agenda for the next action.

All parts are encoded directly and economically.

Text

The following, dated 25th June, is received in Macau from a known trading partner:

> **DEAR TERRY**
>
> **WE ARE INTERESTED IN BUYING STYLE 0310 JACQUARD GIRDLE 1000 DZ: PLEASE ADVISE YOUR BEST PRICE AND DELIVERY?**
>
> **WE ARE ALSO INTERESTED IN OTHER BRAS AND GIRDLES FOR ORDERS: ANY SUGGESTIONS?**
>
> **OUR FAX # 819 876 5416 IN CANADA**
>
> **THANKS & REGS. ALAIN**

The Macau supplier replies immediately, in a more formal manner than he will adopt once a deal is going forward:

DEAR SIR,

THKS FOR YR FAX DD 25-6-1991

ART .0310 V HV ACTUALLY STOPPED PRODUCTION OF THIS ART IN 1990

TO RESTART V NEED A MN OF 3000DOZS, CAN BE IN 3 COLORS. WHITE BEIGE N BLACK

PRICE OF THE ART AS USD 30/70/ DOZ FOR WHITE N BEIGE
USD 32/20/DOZ FOR BLACK

YES, V CAN SEND U SOME SPLS, PL LET US HV YR FULL NAME N ADDRESS.

KINDEST REGARDS

The recipient, himself a native speaker, who had written in a direct laconic English without the abbreviations characteristic of the sender, is expected to understand the following from the fax he receives in reply:

Dear Sir

Th*an*ks for y*ou*r fax d*ate*d 25-6-1991
Art*icle* .0310 *we have* actually stopped production of this Art*icle* in 1990.

To restart *production we* need a *minimum* of 3,000 doz*en*, *production of this item* can be in 3 colors, white, beige, and black
***the* price of the article as USD 30/70/dozen for white *and* beige**
USD 32/20/for black

Yes *we* can send *you* some *samples*, *please* let us *have your* full name *and* address

Kindest regards

Interpretation

The organisation of both faxes is expected and familiar. A discernible and regular, though not invariable, and certainly not a conscious discourse structure can be observed emerging out of business practice. The first in the sequence starts with a request that initiates the exchange: after that the messages adopt the pattern illustrated by the second.

- *Acknowledgement*

  Thanks for your fax dated 25-6-1991

- *Identification*

  Article .0310

- *Unsolicited information*

  ***we have* actually stopped production of this Article in 1990.**
  To restart *production we* need a *minimum* of 3,000 dozen,*production*
  ***of this item* can be in 3 colors, white, beige, and black.**
  ***The* price of the art is USD 30/70 doz for white *and* beige**
  USD 32/20 for black

- *Requested information*

  Yes *we* can send *you* some *samples*.

- *Agenda*

  ***please* let us *have your* full name *and* address.**

Analysis

In this reply there appear other items — an *identification* of the topic, necessary given that the morning's work may involve receiving and responding to many faxes relating to different deals, which may take the simpler and more economical form of: *Re* ... followed by the code number of the deal in question, then an *acknowledgement.* Again this may take the simpler form of *Point 1 — Ntd.* There follows whatever information about that deal necessary for the correspondent to know. This is usually of two kinds: that of *requested information* and *unsolicited information*. The final item is information that relates to the agenda for the next step in the sequence of the transaction. The above example initiates a single deal. It is not necessary to separate out several different deals under identifying headings. Where this is done, each heading is followed by a paragraph having a similar structure of acknowledgement, requested and unsolicited information and agenda, a pattern that may recur several times before the final greeting.

At the level of clause, group and word, correspondents write as directly and clearly as they can and where, as here, their exchanges are confined to immediate matters of forwarding deals, meanings are as a rule satisfactorily encoded.

Those with a native, or a native-like control of the language waste no words and make use of abbreviations they regard as commonly accepted and *only* those. Second language users adopt the highly abbreviated and elliptical style of writing, called here *TradeSpeak*, as if to assert not only the pressure and pace of their working environment, but also to dissociate themselves from attempting the degree of completeness associated with formality, which would challenge their competence, incur criticism, and would at best involve a time-consuming revision process. They rely on their correspondent's ability and willingness to make out the meaning from the clues they offer. By doing so they assert the extent of shared knowledge, and reinforce solidarity of interest.

Of course, errors are made in estimating what is known to a trading partner, but this is well recognised, and direct questions about what is meant, and unmistakable demands for missing information are made. There is a tacit agreement that ambiguities inevitably occur, and must be resolved. Necessary directness is not interpreted as discourtesy. Business negotiation, like the conversation that in some ways it resembles, and the committee meetings supported by associated minutes and agenda with which an analogy has been implied, is a collaborative achievement. The rules of practice in faxed exchanges reflect not conflict of interest but a shared and powerful intention of maximising profit. It is predictable that they will be identified and taught, and that business education will be directed to good practice in them.

There is no support, therefore, in such an interpretation of the faxed correspondence by which deals are accomplished, for the view persuasively argued by Chu (1991) in her book: *The Asian Mind-Game — Unlocking the Hidden Agenda of the Asian Business Culture: a Westerner's Survival Manual.* She undertakes to explain to Western businessmen how it is that East/West negotiations can often be difficult, inconclusive and subject to breakdown. In that view, commerce becomes a contemporary form of combat. The art of war, as it is codified in Chinese classical texts, is the model for Oriental trade negotiation processes. Our observation *is* quite different. Information is shared.

There is a joint interest in achieving a successful deal. Outcomes are, as a rule, reasonably satisfactory to both parties, and business relationships, though occasionally troubled, are typically cordial, and sustained over long periods of time.

5.6 Summary

Study of these exchanges, representative of many, indicates an emerging variety of English that works moderately well, and allows for some flexibility in use, but no more than that. Its rules operate more or less regularly. It demands that the reader should immediately recall a whole apparatus of contextual information, and bring it to bear on the interpretation of what is said. This is usually, but not always, possible. Changes of personnel or simply the passage of time, are likely to obscure much of the meaning, sometimes beyond recall.

There is an emerging variant of English here that develops from experienced needs and meets many of them, but is subject to constant modification. The implications of this last statement are addressed in the following, concluding chapter.

From the point of view of successful trading, there appears to be a risk embodied in the communicative processes to be set against the advantages of speed, familiarity and flexibility. Indications are that the procedures in use are cost-effective, but they are vulnerable to personnel changes. Any change that affects the stability of the workforce would, in addition, destabilise the processes of communication. The small family-based firms that prevail in Hong Kong and Macau make a contribution towards minimising this risk. This form of industrial organisation, often regarded simply as a distinctive cultural feature of Chinese business, could be seen rather as an economic necessity and a functional device to minimise risk: A tightly run ship with few senior crew members who are either family, or have come to be treated as such, ensures that the company and the livelihoods which depend on it, survive.

Conclusion

The concluding section of this book is brief and represents a shift of gear relative to the chapters that precede it. Its purposes are

- to locate this book within related research and antecedents,
- to state its theoretical and practical implications and
- to suggest some possible future developments.

Related Research and Antecedents

The book, and the research activity that preceded it, constitute an interdisciplinary study in the obvious sense of drawing on more than one academic discipline. It is concerned with the informational requirements of international trade proceedings which are part of the subject matter of economics, and with the situated language use, by means of which trade deals are negotiated and brought step by step to completion. The latter is properly the concern of linguistics.

Attention has already been drawn to this new and promising area of enquiry :

> "It is only recently that information has begun to receive the attention from economists that it really deserves. Many insights — theoretical and practical, contemporary and historical — will be derived from the economics of information once the relevant theory becomes better developed." (Casson, 1995a: 1)

The progressively narrowed focus of the book is (in Chapter 4) on trade deals and the agents that mediate them and finally (in Chapter 5), on the retrievable messages they transmit on deals negotiated, implemented and concluded, and on livelihoods earned. This is the observable activity that, in the aggregate, amounts to the extraordinary degree of economic success that is the subject of the two initial chapters.

All this is far removed from the abstractions of those academic disciplines that are, nonetheless, essential to its understanding. Economics reduces the task of coordination to that which takes place through markets, where "market forces", interpreted as known demand and supply, meet. The nature and the cost of those information flows which are required to discover and then to reconcile the demands and supplies are largely ignored. The book belongs, in short, to the study of communications in relation to the functioning of markets, and with reference to their economic significance. A German term that might possibly have developed so as to include such a topic emerged briefly in the 1930s — *Wirtschaftslinguistik* — economic linguistics, but was short-lived, and it seems, judging by the extreme scarcity of references to it, to have evoked no more than transitory interest. We do not propose to revive it, useful as it might be. We should, however, find a suitably descriptive label for the study of language functions in the context of economic activity, the area we have indicated in our title.

We are not isolated in that respect. There is evidence of current interest in the topic and of its gathering momentum in both economics and linguistics. Casson's insistence (1995) on the potential importance for economists on the study of the economics of information attests to it. In his opinion, the conventional theory of the firm has created the fiction of the neo-classical firm,

> "a firm in which the only strategic decision is how to adjust the inputs and outputs to changes in factor and product prices (is) a travesty of the way that the economy actually works. (Casson, 1995a: 4)

The evidence of interest in the topic includes the recent (1990) establishment of the *Journal of Asia Pacific Communication*,[1] which focused, in an early Special Issue, on the subject of language and trade (1991); in the series of recent conferences (organised by the National Centre for English Language Teaching and Research at Macquarie University and the NLLIA Centre for

[1]from July 1997 published by Ablex Publishing Corporation, Greenwich, CT, USA.

Workplace Communication and Culture), of which the most recent (1995) has the title *Local Diversity, Global Connections, Communication, Culture and Business*, and a number of recent publications to which we are heavily indebted and to which reference is made below. Our particular interests are close to being covered by the phrase *Language in the Workplace* — but not without some qualification. Fundamental and recent changes in merchandisers' workplaces, the effect of technological development, are centrally important. Once a merchandiser has constant access to a technology which allows for instant, time-zone independent, and free-format written communication, presently a fax machine, her workplace is changed, as is her use of language in it. A recent survey article entitled *The Death of Distance* makes the point forcefully:

> "The death of distance as a determinant of the cost of communications will probably be the single most important economic force shaping society in the first half of the next century. It will alter, in ways that are only dimly imaginable, decisions about where people live and work; concepts of national borders, patterns of international trade. (The Economist, 1995: 3)

That forecast for the services industry is already a reality in international manufacturing, to which the textile and garment industry — the subject of this study — belongs. Within broadly defined time zones, distance and the costs of bridging it are fast diminishing, and the co-ordination of production and trade changing to an unprecedented degree. Changes in language use are a direct consequence. Rapid interactive exchange, characteristic of verbal communication, is not just possible, but commonplace, in writing, across distances, and independently of time zones. There is nothing new about the emergence, from the context of demanding work, of a restricted variety of English adapted to specific circumstances. (The language of air traffic control and of ship-to-shore communication are obvious examples.) Nor is the idea new that what emerges from work practices can be codified and systematised, and made more effective because of reduced ambiguity, better understood rules, and enhanced ease of learning. The development of *SeaSpeak* again is the best known example.

Meanings verbally encoded in English and transmitted electronically have been the focus of our interest here. The value of faxed transmission however, goes well beyond this use since it can also carry visually encoded meaning (to which only brief reference has been made) and, unlike the telex communication that preceded it, it allows no formatting by the user of a writing system other than the Roman alphabet. The term *Language in the Electronic Work-Place* would serve to formulate this aspect of our interests, and would allow for the fact that fax machines may well be superseded by an extended and developed form, for instance, electronic mail. But the term does little justice to the importance we attach to observing what economists know as transactional processes, recognised as important and too little understood. Fax use makes the negotiations that contribute substantially to these processes observable, and their cost, at least in principle, measurable. Transactions coordinated by language in the electronic work place (though clumsier and longer than we should ideally like) come nearest to locating the subject of our interest.

The most persuasive evidence of a growing recognition of the commonalties of interest between economists and linguists is recent writing about the economic significance of communicative processes. Coulmas' own view of their relationship is one with which we should want to be associated.

> "Linguistics and Economics are not usually seen as neighbouring fields of enquiry, yet there are many common concerns of the two disciplines, and much can be learned from studying these commonalties. The common ground of linguistics and economics is communication. Linguists are concerned to find out how language lends itself to communication, and economists have an interest in making communication efficient." (Coulmas, 1991: 1)

Within this (still restricted in terms of quantity) body of work, we look to Coulmas' own *Language and Economy* (1992) as a classic statement of those commonalties by virtue of its innovativeness, its conceptual grasp, and its comprehensiveness. Coulmas' study examines money and language as social artefacts. It investigates the concept of language as a commodity; it offers a critique of what has been, until recently, an orthodoxy among linguists, the belief that all languages are of equal value to their users. It establishes a basis for the contrary assertion that some languages are *better adapted*, and henceforth, more useful than others, and that their usefulness is in principle a quantifiable asset. It carefully examines the assertion, frequently made, that there is an association between multi-lingualism and poverty of a language. It explains, in terms of its currently vigorous expansion and its exceptional degree of value to its users, the uniquely important international role of English in modern times.

Earlier statements of this concept of language as a commodity, and of the message-bearing character of monetary exchange, occur in the literature of Semiotics. Rossi-Lande takes much further than does Levi-Strauss (1963; 1967) the contention that symbolic systems are inseparable from all except the simplest systems of exchange, arguing in a number of essays (1992) and more fully in an extended monograph, *Linguistics and Economics* (1975), that language and exchange systems should each be considered as semiotic systems, and that there are important identities between their fundamental concepts:

> "when goods circulate in the form of commodities, they are 'messages' and when sentences circulate in the form of verbal messages they are 'commodities'" (Rossi-Lande, 1975: 6)

Products, Rossi-Lande argues, become commodities only in the context of exchange, in becoming messages, and he anticipates the relationship that Coulmas calls *commonalties* in the assertion —

> "Economics offers an excellent model for the study of non-verbal sign systems." (ibidem: 135)

In addition, we are especially indebted to recent studies of the role of verbal communication, of talk, in providing the fundamental framework of social interaction and institutions (Boden and Zimmermann, 1991; Boden, 1994; Friedland and Boden, 1994). These studies demonstrate in detail how conversational interaction is modified in work contexts so as to facilitate the accomplishment of certain tasks. Faxed correspondence can be seen in such terms — as a modification of conversational interchange, and as a mechanism whereby the alignment of views, that is, the essential task of mediation, is accomplished (Friedland and Boden, 1994: 12 *et seq.*). None of this literature identifies as a discipline or a sub-discipline the *commonalties* they investigate. Rather, they engage in investigation and debate concerning them. This book is intended as a contribution to the debate.

Theoretical and Practical Applications

These are summarised under three headings:

- Support for some, and not for other, theoretical positions,
- Recommendations for the extension and use of the data base and
- Advocacy of collaboration between merchandisers and professional linguists.

In locating what we have done, we have already indicated our stance in general terms. We align our work with the belief that developments in technology have brought about a changed context for trade practices; that language use is indispensable to these and makes transactional costs visible, and that a distinctive variety, an operational sub-language of English is currently emerging.

What we have to say can best be expressed in terms of support for some, and not other arguments. A new variety seems to be emerging in response to a fresh set of circumstances — supporting Coulmas' contention that English is a particularly well-adapted language. Our research also provides evidential, and perhaps conceptual, support for the view that the concentration of economics on the price mechanism, as the all-encompassing coordination mechanism for production and exchange, has unacceptable limitations. This has considerable implications for at least two entirely practical issues.

- The teaching of economics, especially at an introductory level, must be revised to include the role of the exchange of non-price information in economic coordination.
- Market-oriented reforms, and the policies employed therein must not only free up prices in order to achieve better allocation, but also to develop the information sector of the economy.

In the practical activity (theoretically motivated) of English Language Teaching for Business Purposes, the research again provides support for assertions that run counter to the orthodoxy. The belief is commonly and often vehemently expressed in Asian countries, for instance in Hong Kong, and recently again in Malaysia, that standards of English are inadequate, and are worsening — a view heavily qualified by those professionally engaged in English Language education. It seems to us to require additional modification on other, and different grounds. Tourists and shoppers are frequently disappointed at the level of listening comprehension and spoken English they encounter.

Merchandisers, who are not usually recruited from among the most successful school students, comprehend and control written English sufficiently well for the varied and demanding purposes. The working environment provides incentive, opportunity and limited targets. It is inevitable that demands of language learning on the time of students will increase, with additional and understandable pressure to establish Asian languages such as *Putonghua* (Mandarin) or Bahasa Malay as first languages. In terms of language learning policy, our research supports the view that

- English is indispensable to export-orientated development;
- an all-round level of competence in English may be an unrealistic target within the secondary school curriculum; and
- additional resources should go to work-related language study at tertiary and post-tertiary levels.

In terms of the study of international business, the research does not support the belief that Chinese, as opposed to Western, business persons conceptualise trade proceedings as a form of combat. (Chu, 1991). On the contrary, our evidence suggests that typically they perceive buyers and sellers as dependent on agents for successful coordination of production and trade in a joint enterprise. Nor is it, in our view, the case that typically they take a short-term view of outcomes — on the contrary, the long-term business relationship is regarded as more significant than the outcome of a particular deal.

The need for a collection, or archive, or database, related to the transaction of business is already authoritatively recognised. (Coase, 1992) As a contribution towards this end, the data underlying this research project have been made accessible at the New Zealand Social Science Research Data and Information Services Centre, and through them, via the Internet at the Massey University home page (http://www.massey.ac.nz). Its content, arrangement, its mode of assembly and its limitations are described, and it is our intention to make it available to researchers, and to those writers of materials and curriculum designers who would welcome access to a body of authentic materials.

A Final Remark

The intention of this book, and of the research that preceded it, was to contribute to an understanding of the extraordinary success of Hong Kong and Macau, exemplars of high performing East Asian economies. From a study which starts with the generalities that can be inferred from statistical information and narrows by stages to scrutiny of the details of the workdays of those who negotiate trade deals, a number of significant factors emerge. One is the crucial importance of individuals' control of an international language — a control that is certainly not the attainment of an even bilingualism. Another is the availability of a carrier of information, speedy, free-format, affordable, independent of time zones, and independent of high levels of proficiency in pronunciation and listening comprehension. At present, facsimile transmission meets these requirements. Electronic mail (or a successor of electronic mail) may, in future, replace fax. It is the co-occurrence of these two conditions — the one brought about by developments in technology, the other the effect of developed educational systems — that makes each of them economically so significant. It is almost as if to the existing and well-known criteria for successful, newly industrialising economies might be added, not an additional criterion, but a facilitating condition, present in the NIEs, namely:

- widespread literacy in a language that goes beyond national and cultural boundaries; and
- an available technology that permits the rapid transmission, across distance, of written text accompanied by visual illustration.

Communication has proved to be the essential factor in that success. An international language and the means of rapid transmission have made that communication possible.

Governments can and do choose policies that promote or inhibit these conditions.

Appendix

Yachtsman Jersey 3

LookOut (Macau) trading with the French buying office in Hong Kong
Transcribed text of a sequence of faxes
June–November 1993

No.1

Date 28th May 1993

Sender Catherine for LookOut

Receiver Heidi/Cindy for the French buying office

<u>Re Spot Mens Dept New Orders '94</u>

A) Polo Ben 7 boutons

Pls be infmd tt the pcs smpl of abv bref tt v snt u /re in fab qlty of 100% cotton 2x2 rib melange grey but in 310 g/m2 as v could not find avail fab in 200 g/m2 pls be kind enough to infm client. thks .

B) Tunisien ml basic

pls note tt v shll snd u a piece of the melange fabric tomm for yr reference as smpls were made in soild color jersey.

C) Polo Rugby in print stripe sand washed

Further to yr phone call, yr client's target px of USD 6.60/pc is really not acptble, in fact o/ quoted px in o/office of USD 7.20/pc is really o/ best px . in any case, after negotiation with o/factory, the best v can do is USD 7.10/pc.pls convey this px of ours to yr client. thks.

D) Polo Rugby cut & sewn with hidden placket

same situation as abv point C, after much effort to convince o/factory, v came to o/bst px of USD 6.55/pc

thks to take note of the abv.

B. Rgds.

No. 2

Date 16th June 1993

Sender Cindy for the French buying office

Receiver Catherine for LookOut

Re Yachtsman Jersey 3

The sent counter sample was rcvd + comments as below:-
- style: ok
- weight: we prefer *(Note 1)* to keep the weight as yr sample 310 gm/m2 1/0 original in 280 gm /m2 for production .

collar & cuff: We want the collar & cuff with spandex not as yr smpl.
measurement: 1) ok for the cut & sewn on sleeve & bottom but pls modify the measurement as follows

(Annotated sketch inserted.)

2) other measurement are ok.
- We would like an half-moon back as next page

(photo-copied fabric with annotation attached on a separate page)

Pls send us a new smpl with print stripe in 3x4 cm as enclosed page *(Note 2)* + above -mentioned modification

Thanks to inform the smpl delivery date

B. Rgds.

(Sketch of two rectangles labelled by hand — No wash Stone wash.)

Note 1: There is a hand written note before printed stripes. *It is not possible to know whether this was an afterthought by the sender or a note by the receiver.*
Note 2: We do not have the enclosed page mentioned.

No. 3

Date 18th June 1993

Sender Cindy for the French buying office

Receiver Catherine for LookOut

Re Yachtsman Jersey 3

After clarify with our buyer ,the additional sample comments is as belos:

- we need the effect instone washed/print stripe, but prefer the handfeel more hard than your smpl.
- weight - 320 gm/m 2 (after print stripe + stone washed)
- the print stripe in navy - 4 cm
- " " white - 3 cm

(Annotated sketch)

S *(shoulder measurement)* = 18 cm
Q *(welt)* = 15 cm is forall the size

Pls re-quote us the price with print stripe + stone-washed efect for this style.

B. Rgds.

No. 4

Date 18th June 1993

Sender Catherine for LookOut

Receiver Cindy for the French buying office

Re Yachtsman Jersey 3

Re yr fax 7140 dd 18/6/93. Aftr checking w/o factory, v hv to infm tt stone wash cannot be applied onto the French rib garment as it will ruin the garment, in place of stone wash, v were ifmd by the factory tt v cld get heavy sand wash which will have the similar effect as stone wash.

In the mtime, since yr client now requires 320G/M2 (after print wash), v shll hv to re-quote u a new px to accomodate these changes and r as follws:-

- USD 11.75/pc (w 320G/M2 aftr print + heavy sand wash)
- USD 11.05/pc (w 320G /M2 aftr print)

Thks to confirm if abv is okay. The revised sample in printed stripes shall be avail in 12 days time.

B. Rgds.

No. 5

Date 21st July 1993

Sender Catherine for LookOut

Receiver the French buying office

Spot Men Knit *(handwritten note: 10/8/93–30*
10/9/93
10/10/93–30
3/11/93)

I <u>Re Yachtsman Jersey 3</u>

Referring to the abv item, hv contacted factory n was ifmd of the llwg:-

- fab qlty:100% cotton French rib. 320 g/m2 aftr print + heavy sand wash
- px: USD 11.30 pc
- sz: s/m/l/xl
- quota : EEC 4 to France
- shipmt: 5/11/93 subjt to recvg full order dtls such as qties, color assortment, mk-up etc. by 5/8/93
- mk-up: normal mk-up *(hand written note: 50 days)*
- FOB (+quota) HongKong; L/C at sight.

All qties, shipmt are subjt to final confirmation.

II <u>Polo Ben with 7 buttons</u> in melange grey 200 g/m2

Factory is chkg on shmt and avail fab swatch, shll rvt tomm latest. thks.

No. 6

Date 21st July 1993

Sender Cindy for the French buying office

Receiver Catherine for LookOut

<u>Re Yachtsman Jersey 3</u>

The rvd smpl was rcvd + comments as below
- style: OK
- weight: OK
- washing effect: OK
- stripe: OK

half mn back: OK, but we want *(Inserted sketch shows depth of 9 cm)*
meas of cut & sewn "S" s/b - 18 cm not 16 cm as yr smpl.
"Q" s/b -15 cm not 14 cm as yr smpl (n.1)

other meas: armhole – s/b 27 cm not 28 cm
cuff rib – s/b 3.5 cm not 3 cm
neck width – s/b 20 cm not 24 cm
neck drop – s/b 4 cm not 3 cm
body length – s/b 72 cm not 75 cm. *(Note 1)*

color: OK for navy & white - however we prefer to change the part of plain color on cut & sewn + cuff + collar rib in navy i/o whiteas yr smpl. Pls refer to the drawing as next page

(Inserted sketch shows distribution of striped and plain fabric)

Finally, pls be reminded to take care of the meas.in bulk production & pls follow our size spec+ meas.instruction exactly.

B. Rgds.

Note 1. In these detailed amendments to the size, "S" and "Q" refer to the shoulder and welt dimensions identified in this way in the diagram on page 3. The abbreviation s/b *is* "should be".

No. 7

Date 22nd July 1993

Sender Cindy for the French buying office

Receiver Catherine for LookOut

Re Yachtsman Jersey 3

- price: USD 11.30 — OK
- shipmt: 5/11/93 — OK
- size/co in breakdown:

navy/wh combination	S	M	L	XL	
	160	340	340	160	= 1000 pcs

B. Rgds.

No. 8

Date 23rd July 1993

Sender Catherine for LookOut

Receiver Heidi for the French buying office

RE Spot Men Knit - Yachtsman Jersey 3

Re yr fax 8170 dd 22 /7/93

Hv chkd w/ factory and cfmd the fllwg:-

- fab qlty: 100% cotton French rib, 320 gm/m2 *(over written 400 gm/m2)*
- qties: 1000 pcs in one colorway
- px: USD 11.30/pc (pls note tt o/quoted px is based on o/smpl i.e. the plain color part is to be white. Hever, since yr client rqstd the plain color part to be navy, xtra costs is involved, but since this is the 1st order w/spot men knit, v shll not increase the px)
- shpt: 5/11/93
- quota E.E.C. 4 to France
- mk-up: normal mk-up, xtra accessories such as woven lbl+ hang-tag will be subjt to xtra charges
- terms: FOB (+quota) HongKong: L/C at sight.

Pls note tt factory has made a mistake and v were ifmd tt the smpl tt v snt is in fact of weight 400 gm/m2 and not the rqstd 320 g/m2. But v shll correct for 320 g/m2 for bulk prdtn.

Chkg w/factory when v can snd pre-production smpl.will ifm later. Thks to snd o/s asap.

B. Rgds.

No. 9

Date 27th July 1993

Sender Cindy for the French buying office

Receiver Catherine for LookOut

Re Yachtsman Jersey 3

The care/size labelas mentioned below was OK by buyer:

100% coton
TAILLE S — M, L, XL

(International care symbols inserted)

Besides, pls put the care/size label on side seam & main label on neck seam as below

(Sketch indicates exact positions where labels should be attached.)

With reference tothe tel. conversation between Heidi & Catherine, it is confirmed to keep the same quality weight as counter sample that approved by buyer and at price USD 11.30.

Order sheet will be issued accordingly.

B. Rgds.

No. 10

Date 5th August 1993

Sender Catherine for LookOut

Receiver Cindy for the French buying office

<u>Re Yachtsman Jersey 3</u>

Further to yr fax dd 27/7/93, v hv alrdy proceeded with fabric production, so shll ifm of avail of pre-production smpl much later.

Hever as per phone call w/Cindy, found tt yr client rqstd this item to be shppd under E.E.C. cat.4 (pls refer to o/fax 931441 dd 23/7/93.)

v hv actually gone up to Macau authorities with the smpl, and they cfmd tt item is under cat.4, so pls ask yr client to clarify whether item is under cat.4 and cat.5

In any case, if yr client insist to ship under cat.5, then as u wellknow, cat.5 costs more than cat.4, so an xtra cost of USD 0.50/pc is involved so final px is at USD 11.80/pc.

Pls ugtly repy by rtn as v hv alrdy started the production of fabric and v need ananswer in order to get quota costs as quota costs fluctuate quite a bit (it might affect o/now quoted px of USD 11.80/pc) thks to clarify w/yr client .

B. Rgds.

No. 11

Date 9th August 1993

Sender Catherine for LookOut

Receiver Cindy for the French buying office

Re Yachtsman Jersey 3

Further to o/fax 931551 dd 5/8/93 and phone call between Cindy/Catherine, understood tt yr client is willing to xtra USD 0.40/pc i/o 0.50/pc forshipping this item under E.E.C 5 to France.

Even though the xta USD 0.4/pc is not enough to cover the quota cost for E.E.C. 5, v, nevertheless, cfm to acpt the xtra charge of USDO.40/pc since this is the first orderfor Spot MenKnit.

So final px for this item is at USD 11.70/pc FOB + Quota HongKong; L/C atsight. Othr terms remain unchanged as per o/fax 931441 dd 23/7/93

B. Rgds.

No. 12

Date 18th September 1993

Sender Cindy for the French buying office

Receiver Catherine for LookOut

Re Yachtsman Jersey 3

The bulk fabric swatches dd 13/9 was OK for lor *(sic)* & washing effect & collar rib.

B. Rgds.

No. 13

Date 18th September 1993

Sender Cindy for the French buying office

Receiver Catherine for LookOut

Re Yachtsman Jersey 3/your fax pt.A dd 6/10/93 *(Note 1)*

Noted

However, we don't have keep sample in our side as you sent only one pc of collar rib to us, so we presumed you will follow the same rib for production as approved.

B. Rgds.

Note 1. The fax of this date, to which this is an immediate reply, is not in our collection.

No. 14

Date 14th October 1993

Sender Cindy for the French buying office

Receiver Catherine for LookOut

Re Yachtsman Jersey 3

The pre-production sample was rcvd & comments by buyer as below:-
- measurement: OK for size S. however
  .neck drop: s/b 4m not 1cm
  .shoulder: s/b 20 cm not 19 cm

- stitching: For double stitching below collar, we would like in white i/o navy as the sent sample.
  Besides, we prefer single stitching in white on half moon back i/o double stitching in navy.

Pls go on for bulk production.

No. 15

Date 4th November 1993

Sender Catherine for LookOut

Receiver Cindy for the French buying office

Re Spot Order Yachtsman Jersey 3

Further to Cindy's inspection on 2/11/93 v hv re-inspected the goods and hereby re-confirm the fllwg:-

- all carton labels hv been filled in w/carton numbers
- all garments hv been re-packed into export cartons aftr chkg for loose threads and dirt on garment at random

v therefore ask u to release the shpmt and snd us the inspection certificate in order for us to reserve booking w/shipping company as shipment for this order is scheduled on 5/11/93 and closing date for this shpmt is tomorrow 5/11/93. Thks.

B. Rgds.

No. 16

Date 4th November 1993

Inspection Certificate

Buyer: Spot Men's Dept. (Name of French Importer)
Supplier Look Out
Order No. 941 17 0224 (Yachtsman Jersey 3)
shipped by sea
Quantity 952 pcs.

The inspection has been carried out at random and generally applies only to part of the total quantity released for shipment. The issue of this inspection has no effect on the rights of Aydey Group/our Principal to claim any deviations in the goods released for shipment when compared with the conditions contained in the order .

HK Buying Office

Date 4 Nov '93

List of References

Almanac of Macau's Economy 1984–1986 (1986), Macau: *Jornal Va Kio*.

Asia Yearbook 1994: A Review of Events of 1993, ed. by Delfs, R (1993), Hong Kong: Review Publishing Company.

Boden, D (1994) *The Business of Talk: Organisations in Action*, London: Polity Press.

Boden, D and D H Zimmermann (1991) *Talk and Social Structure*, London: Polity Press.

Boxer, C R (1959) *The Great Ship from Amacon. Annals of Macao and the Old Japan Trade, 1555–1640*, Lisbon: Centro de Estudos Historicos Ultramarinos.

Boxer, C R (1965) *Portuguese Societies in the Tropics. The Municipal Councils of Goa, Macao, Bahia, and Luanda*, 1510–1800, Madison, Mil.: University of Wisconsin Press.

Casson, M (1995) "Information and Economc Organisation", *Discussion Papers in Economics*, No. 317, University of Reading.

Casson, M (1995a) "The Process of Coordination", *Discussion Papers in Economics*, No. 318, University of Reading.

Cencig, E (1990) "United Colours: Colour Terms in Contemporary Fashion Trends", *International Journal of LSP, Research, Didactics, and Terminology*, Vol.12, Nos. 3–4, 114–128.

Chen, E K Y (1979) *Hyper-Growth in Asian Economies: A Comparative Study of Hong Kong, Japan, Korea, Singapore, and Taiwan*, New York: Holmes & Meier.

Chu, C N (1991) *The Asian Mind Game: Unlocking the Hidden Agenda of the Asian Business Culture — A Westerner's Guide to Survival*, New York: Rawson Associates.

Cicourel, A V (1988) "Text and Context: Cognitive, Linguistic, and Organisational Dimensions in International Negotiations", *Negotiation Journal*, (July 1988), 257–266.

Clavell, J (1966) *Taipan*, Coronet Books.

Cline, W R (1982) "Can the East Asian Model of Development Be Generalised?" *World Development* 10 (2), (February 1982), 81–99.

Coase, R H (1992) "The Institutional Structure of Production", *American Economic Review*, Vol.82, No.4, 713–719.

Coates, A (1966) *Prelude to Hong Kong*, London: Routledge and Kegan Paul.

Coates (1978) *A Macao Narrative*, Hong Kong: Heinemann Educational Books.

Cope, B and N Solomon (1993) "Workplace Implications of the National Adult Language, Literacy, and Numeracy Competence Framework" *International Conference: Communication in the Workplace: Culture, Language, and Organisational Change*, 1–4 September 1993, Sydney.

Coulmas, F (1991) "The Language Trade in the Asian Pacific", *Journal of Asian Pacific Communication*, Vol.2, No.1, 1–27.

Coulmas, F (1992) *Language and Economy*, London: Blackwell.

Cremer, R D (1991) "From Portugal to Japan: Macau's Place in the History of World Trade", Cremer, R D (ed.) *Macau: City of Commerce and Culture*, 2nd ed., Hong Kong: API Press, 23–38.

Cremer, R D (1991a) "Chinese Entrepreneurs and Enterprises: Microfoundations of Export-oriented Industrialisation" Cremer, R D (ed.) *Macau: City of Commerce and Culture*, 2nd ed., Hong Kong: API Press, 201–220.

Cremer, R D and M J Willes (1991) "Stock in Trade: The Role of English in International Trade Proceedings", *Journal of Asian Pacific Communication*, Vol.2, No.1, 103–116.

Cremer, R D and M J Willes (1994) "Overcoming Language Barriers to Internatonal Trade: A Text-Based Study of the Language of Deals", *Journal of Asian Pacific Communication*, Vol.5, No.3, 147–161.

Dahrendorf, R (1979) "Lebenschancen. Dimensionen der Freiheit in Gesellschaft" [Life Chances. Dimensions of Freedom in Society], in Dahrendorf, R (1979) *Lebenschancen. Anlaeufe zur sozialen und politischen Theory [Life Chances. Approaches to Social and Political Theory*], Frankfurt am Main: Suhrkamp Taschenbuch Verlag.

Edmonds, R L (1994) "Population and Development in Macau: An Introduction" Ramos R et al., (eds.), *Population and Development in Macau*, Macau: University of Macau Publication Centre.

Ellis, M and C Johnson (1994) *Teaching Business English*, Oxford: Oxford University Press.

Fairclough, N (1993) *Discourse and Social Change*, London: Polity Press.

Feitor, R and R D Cremer (1991) "Macau's Modern Economy" Cremer, R D (ed.) *Macau: City of Commerce and Culture*, 2nd ed., Hong Kong: API Press, 183–199.

Friedland, R and D Boden (1994) *Nowhere, Space, and Modernity Time*, University of California Press.

Fuchs, V R (1994) "Nobel Laureate: Gary S. Becker: Ideas about Facts" *Journal of Economic Perspectives*, (Spring 1994), 183–192.

Giles, H (1977) *Language, Ethnicity, Intergroup Relations*, London: Academic Press.

Giles, H and P F Powesland (1975) *Speech Style and Social Evaluation*, London: Academic Press.

Glover, A *et al.* (1987) *SeaSpeak Reference Manual*, International Civil Aviation Organisation, Document 9432.

Grimwade, N (1989) International Trade: New Patterns of Trade, Production and Investment, London and New York: Routledge.

Gross, B M (1966) "The State of the Nation: Social Systems Accounting" in Bauer, R A, ed., *Social Indicators*, Cambridge Mass., 154–271.

Haberler, G (1988) *International Trade and Economic Development*, San Francisco: International Center for Economic Growth.

Hayek, F A (1936), "Economics and Knowledge", Presidential address delivered before the London Economic Club, November 10, 1936, in Hayek, F A, *Individualism and Economic Order*, London and Henley: Routledge and Kegan Paul (reprinted in 1976 from *Economica* IV (new series, 1937), 33–56.

Hong Kong Statistics 1947–1967 (1969) Census and Statistics Department, Hong Kong.

Institute of Developing Economies (1984–1990), *Changes in the Industrial Structure and the Role of Small and Medium Industries in Asian Countries*, Institute of Developing Economies, Economic Development Research Unit, Tokyo.

James, D L (1995), *The Executive Guide to Asia-Pacific Communications*, New York, Tokyo, and London: Kodansha International.

James, W E, Naya, S, and G M Meier (1987) *Asian Development: Economic Success and Policy Lessons*, San Francisco: International Center for Economic Growth.

Juster, F T (1971) *A Framework of the Measurement of Economic and Social Performance*, New York: National Bureau of Economic Research.

Julian, M J (1990) *Bargaining Across Boundaries*, unpublished Ph.D. Thesis, University of Edinburgh.

Kuznets, S (1973) "Modern Economic Growth: Findings and Reflections" (Nobel Lecture), *American Economic Review*, Vol.63 (September 1973).

Knight, F (1941) "Review of Melvill J. Hersovits' 'Economic Anthropology'" *Journal of Political Economy*, 49 (April 1941), 246– 258, quoted by Milgrom, P and J Roberts (1992) *Economics, Organisation and Management*, Englewood Cliffs N.J.: Prentice Hall: 19.

Landsberg, M (1987), "Export-led Industrialisation in the Third World: Manufacturing Imperialism" Peet, R (ed.), *International Capitalism and Industrial Restructuring*, Boston: Allen and Unwin.

Levinson, S R (1983), *Pragmatics*, Cambridge: Cambridge University Press.

Levi-Strauss, C (1963) *Structural Anthropology I*, (translated by C Jacobson and B Grundfest Schoepf, New York: Basic Books Inc.

Levi-Strauss, C (1967) *Structural Anthropology II*, translated by M Layton, Harmondsworth: Penguin Books.

Lin, T B and M C Lin (1979), "Exports and Employment in Hong Kong" Lin T B, Lee, R P L, and U E Simonis (eds.), *Hong Kong: Economic, Social and Political Studies in Development*, New York: M E Sharpe, 225–273.

Meadows, D *et al.* (1972), *The Limits to Growth*, New York 1972.

Milgrom, P and Roberts, J (1992) *Economics, Organisation and Management*, Englewood Cliffs, N.J.: Prentice Hall.

Mill, J S (1848) *Principles of Political Economy, with some of their Applications to Social Philosophy*, Vol. I and II, London: J W Parker, (Facsimile).

MFAT Ministry of Foreign Affairs and Trade (1995) *Hong Kong: Information Paper*, Wellington: March 1995.

Mo, T (1986) *An Insular Possession*, London: Picador.

Montalto de Jesus, C A (1926) *Historic Macau: International Traits in China, Old and New*, 2nd ed., Macau: Salesian Printing Press.

Ormerod, P (1994) *The Death of Economics*, London: Faber and Faber.

Pires, B V (1991) "Origins and Early History of Macau" Cremer, R D (ed.) *Macau: City of Commerce and Culture*, 2nd ed., Hong Kong: API Press, 7–21.

Rajapatirana, S (1987) "Industrialisation and Foreign Trade: What is the Relationship between Industrialisation, Trade, and Economic Performance?", *Finance and Development* (September 1987).

Rossi-Lande, F (1975) *Linguistics and Economics*, The Hague: Mouton.

Rossi-Lande, F, ed. (1992) *Between Signs and Non-Signs*, Amsterdam and Philadelphia: John Benjamin's Publishing Co.

Sit, V F S, Cremer, R D, and S L Wong (1991) *Entrepreneurs and Enterprises in Macau: A Study of Industrial Development*, Hong Kong: Hong Kong University Press and API Press.

Sit, V F S and S L Wong (1989) *Small and Medium Industries in an Export-oriented Economy: The Case of Hong Kong*, Centre of Asian Studies, University of Hong Kong.

Sit, V F S and S L Wong (1990) Small-Medium Industries and Entrepreneurship in China: Case Study of Guangdong Province, unpublished Research Report, Hong Kong, University of Hong Kong.

Smith, A (1776) *An Inquiry into the Nature and the Causes of the Wealth of Nations*, Vol. I and II, London: Strahan and Cadell, (Facsimile).

Spence, J D (1985) *The Memory Palace of Matteo Ricci*, London and Boston: Faber and Faber.

The Economist (1995), The Death of Distance: A Survey of Telecommunications, *The Economist*, 30 Sept 1995.

Thorndyke, P W (1977) "Cognitive Structures in Comprehension and Memory of Narrative Discourse" *Cognitive Psychology* 9, 77–110.

Todaro, M P (1994) *Economic Development*, 5th ed., Essex: Longman Group.

Toward a Social Report (1970), The U.S. Department of Health, Education, and Welfare, Ann Arbor, Washington.

Toward Balanced Growth (1970), Report of the National Goals Research Staff, Washington 1970.

Tsuru S, (1993) *Japan's Capitalism: Creative Defeat and Beyond*, Cambridge: Cambridge University press.

UNDP (1990) *Human Development Report 1990*, United Nations Development Programme, New York, Oxford: Oxford University Press.

Waring, M (1988), *Counting for Nothing*, Wellington: Allen and Unwin N.Z.

White Paper on the World Economy (1994), Overseas Research Division, Research Bureau, Economic Planning Agency, Government of Japan, Tokyo.

Williamson, O E (1989) "Transaction Cost Economics", in Schmalensee, R and R D Willig, eds., *Handbook of Industrial Organisation*, Vol.1, Amsterdam: Elsevier 1989, 136–182.

Wong, S L (1986) "Modernisation and Chinese Culture in Hong Kong", *China Quarterly* 106 (June 1986), 306–325.

Wong, S L (1988) *Emigrant Entrepreneurs: Shanghai Industrialists in Hong Kong*, Hong Kong: Oxford University Press.

World Bank (1988) *World Development Report 1988: Opportunities and Risks in Managing the World Economy*, New York, Oxford: Oxford University Press.

World Bank (1990) *World Development Report 1990: Poverty*, New York, Oxford: Oxford University Press.

World Bank (1993) *World Development Report 1993: Investing in Health*, New York, Oxford: Oxford University Press.

World Bank (1993a) *The East Asian Miracle: Economic Growth and Public Policy*, World Bank Policy Research Report, New York, Oxford: Oxford University Press.

World Bank (1995) *World Development Report 1995: Workers in an Integrating World*, New York, Oxford: Oxford University Press.

Zagorin, A (1995) "Real Wealth of Nations", *Time*, 2 Oct 1995:35.

Access to the Database

The Secretary of the
Centre for Applied Economics and Policy Studies
(Director: Professor A N Rae)
College of Business
Massey University
Palmerston North
New Zealand

Ph: +64-6-350 5354
Fx: +64-6-350 5660
E-mail: J.Fisher@massey.ac.nz

Index